PAUL AND THE WORLD'S MOST FAMOUS LETTERS

PAUL AND THE WORLD'S MOST FAMOUS LETTERS

Rosemary Haughton

*First published in 1969 by Geoffrey Chapman Limited,
London, as WHY THE EPISTLES WERE WRITTEN, copyright
© 1969, Rosemary Haughton. U.S. edition printed
by arrangement with Geoffrey Chapman Limited.*

Photographs by Herbert G. May with following
exceptions:
page 8 by Three Lions Inc.; page 10 by the Ameri-
can Bible Society; page 11 by Smithsonian Institution, Freer Gallery of Art; page 22 by Don B.
Parkinson; page 25 by Richard T. Lee; page 29
by Israel Office of Information; page 31 by the
William Thompson Literary and Photo Service
(G. Eric Matson); page 40 by Nash, from Three
Lions; page 46 by H. Thomas Frank; page 56 by
Schalek, from Three Lions; page 65 by J. Lane
Miller; page 67 by H. Thomas Frank; page 69 by
Publishers Photo Service; page 75 by Israel Office
of Information; page 76 by Toge Fujihira, Meth-
odist Missions; page 81 by Israel Office of Informa-
tion; page 90 by Publishers Photo Service; page
95 by Herman H. Kreider; page 102 by J. Lane
Miller; page 105 by Three Lions.

contents

1. Corinth—The Unlikely Church *13*
2. How Paul Wrote to Thessalonica *19*
3. The Day of the Lord *24*
4. "Are You Mad, Galatians?" *30*
5. Bad News from Corinth *38*
6. The Foolish Corinthians *44*
7. In Chains for Christ *51*
8. Earthenware Jars *57*
9. Paul to the Romans *64*
10. Faith and Law *71*
11. How Paul's Plans Were Upset *78*
12. Paul at the Heart of the Empire *85*
13. A Letter to the Gentiles *94*
14. The Church Founded on the Apostles *101*
    Other Helpful Books 107
    Index 109

NOTE TO THE READER

While this edition is not intended as a text-book, its subject is one that lends itself to study. At the end of each chapter there are suggestions for further study. These can be used by a teacher in a classroom situation or by the interested reader who wants a better understanding and more knowledge of Paul and his letters and teachings.

It is also important to read the New Testament texts. Consult Young Readers Bible, *edited by Henry M. Bullock and Edward C. Peterson (A. J. Holman Company, Philadelphia, 1965; Abingdon Press, distributors). Two other translations which are helpful are* Good News for Modern Man: The New Testament in Today's English Version, *edited by R. G. Bratcher (American Bible Society, New York, 1966) and* The New Testament in Modern English, *translated by J. B. Phillips (Macmillan, New York, 1958).*

Suggestions for other helpful books can be found on page 107.

The fiery zeal of Paul's preaching is captured by the sculptor Bernini, in the Lateran Basilica

introduction

The most famous letters in the history of the world are the ones we know as the "letters of Paul." You may have seen them in the Bible or heard them read in church, and perhaps been rather bored by them and wondered why they were so important. This book is not the story of Paul's life but an account of how, why, where and when he wrote his letters. So it starts in the middle of his life, since for a good deal of his life he didn't write any letters—or, if he did, they have been lost, and we know nothing about them.

Paul lived in the first century A.D. He wrote two kinds of letters —the kind we usually call a letter, addressed to a single person and meant to be read only by him. There is only one of this kind for certain in the Bible. The other kind was for a lot of people to read: it was meant to be read aloud, handed round, copied, kept. This kind of *"epistole,"* as it was called, was written by quite a number of famous writers and scholars of ancient Greece and Rome. They were meant to be published, almost like a book, and most of Paul's letters are of this kind.

If we want to read Paul's letters or epistles today, we find them collected together with other books and letters in the New Testament, which has been put with the Old Testament to form the Bible. (The Bible is not a single book but a *collection* of books which the early Church thought were special.)

HOW THE WRITING WAS DONE

The history of the letters is probably something like this. Paul dictated a letter to a secretary, who wrote on a primitive kind of paper called "papyrus," which was made from thick reeds that were stripped down, put in two layers, and pressed together. For a pen the secretary used a reed with a sharpened point at the end, and he would have some spare pens to use when the point became blunt, which often happened. His ink was black, and usually made from black stuff called carbon. In many ways he was like someone today in an office or classroom doing dictation, but there are two big differences. He didn't sit at an ordinary table as we do, but

9

stood and wrote, or sat on a stool or bench (or even on the ground) with his papyrus on his knees. Also he did not take down dictation word for word, but often decided the exact words of the letter himself, while Paul gave him the ideas and wrote a short message at the end. (Look up Paul's short message at the end of the first letter to the Corinthians, and the end of the letters to the Galatians, Colossians, and 2 Thessalonians.)

After a letter had been written and signed, it was rolled up and sealed and sent off. Later, when the early Church saw that Paul's letters were very important for everyone to read and not just for the people or groups they were first sent to, the early Christians collected and copied Paul's letters. They had them put on long rolls of papyrus which were wound round stocks and rods (sort of like the scrolls of the Hebrew Law). A roll of papyrus was about nine inches wide and long enough (over thirty feet) to take several of Paul's letters (to give you an idea of the length, the book of Acts probably took up one single roll).

The trouble was that a long roll of papyrus was clumsy to handle and it was hard to find one's place in it. About A.D. 100 or soon after, Christians had the idea of putting pieces of papyrus together in the form of pages and sewing them together. This meant that all Paul's letters (and all the Gospels, too) could be put into one book. As time went by, Paul's letters were copied many times and put together in this way with the rest of the books of the Bible.

At first the writing was very dense, and there were often not even any spaces between words, or periods and commas. To help the reader, some copyists or scribes—the people who copied the manuscripts or handwritten texts of the Bible—put in chapter numbers and explanatory notes in the margin, or at the top where they put in a chapter break.

When you look at your Bible today, you will see it is divided into chapters and verses. These divisions were made up many hundreds of years after Paul lived —the chapters were probably numbered in the thirteenth century and the verses in the sixteenth.

Smithsonian Institution,
Freer Gallery of Art
A third-century Egyptian manuscript showing Greek writing on papyrus

TO KNOW PAUL BETTER

To learn more about Paul's letters, list the materials used for letter writing in Paul's time. Learn how paper was made. Find examples of the kind of handwriting used for the letters and practice this handwriting. Examine a picture of a letter of Paul's time written in Greek.

Learn the names of other famous letter writers of ancient Greece and Rome.

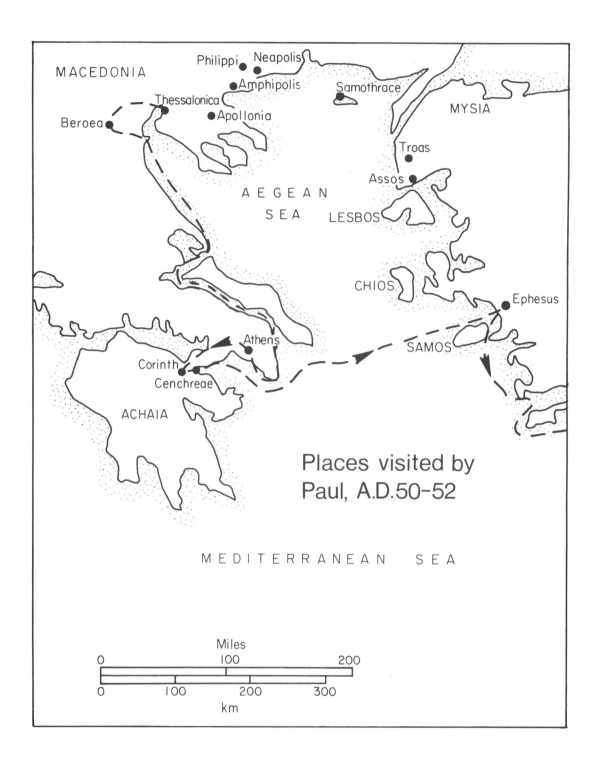

MACEDONIA

Philippi ● Neapolis ●

Amphipolis ●

Thessalonica ●

Beroea ● ● Apollonia

Samothrace ●

MYSIA

Troas ●

Assos ●

A E G E A N
S E A

LESBOS

CHIOS

Ephesus ●

Athens ●

SAMOS

Corinth ●
Cenchreae ●

ACHAIA

Places visited by
Paul, A.D.50–52

M E D I T E R R A N E A N   S E A

Miles
0   100   200

0   100   200   300
km

1 Corinth—The Unlikely Church

One day in A.D. 50, Paul of Tarsus reached Corinth. He sailed from the deep blue Aegean Sea into the harbor of the noisy, smelly and busy port of Cenchreae. When he landed, he found himself among men of every kind—black, fair-skinned, brown, speaking all kinds of languages. He made his way inland to the great city of Corinth itself.

Herbert G. May
The ruins of the temple of Apollo give the modern observer a glimpse into the past of Corinth, one of the richest and most beautiful cities of ancient Greece

Paul arrived in Corinth by himself, for he had left his two friends Timothy and Silas behind in Thessalonica, when he had to leave there in a hurry. It was becoming almost a habit with Paul to leave in a hurry. The message he preached made some of his audience ask eagerly for baptism, but it made others wild with rage and he often had to flee for his life.

This time his preaching in Thessalonica and another town called Beroea had caused such a row that the Christians who lived there were afraid for his safety. They put Paul on a boat bound for Athens, with a companion to show him where to go. He tried preaching in Athens, and he converted a few people there, but most of the Athenians thought he was a bit mad. They liked leisurely, cool arguments, in which the reasons for things were worked out step by step, but Paul was asking them to change their lives, because Jesus Christ had overcome death. It seemed nonsense to them. So Paul left Athens and went on to Corinth by himself.

CORINTH IN THE FIRST CENTURY A.D.

Paul soon realized that Corinth was going to be a tough place to convert, too. In fact no one but Paul would have thought of trying, for Corinth had the worst reputation of any city in the Roman Empire. If you look at the map of the Mediterranean on page 72, it will help you to see why Corinth was likely to be a shady, tough sort of place. Many of the main trade routes between Rome and Asia Minor went through Corinth. Instead of sailing all the way round the Greek peninsula, ships sailed up the Gulf of Corinth. At Lechaeon the bigger boats unloaded, and sent their goods overland to Cenchreae on the Saronic Gulf, but small boats were hauled, cargo and all, from one port to another by a slipway, called the "Dialkos," about four miles long.

But not all goods went straight on through the Gulf. Many were brought to Corinth and sold there to merchants who would send them on again, using their own ships, or sending them overland by the magnificent Roman roads. So Corinth was a great market as well as a stopping place for sailors and merchants and travelers. Corinth didn't have any industries of its own, except for a souvenir industry. All its riches came from the trade that passed through it —and it was an enormously rich city. Corinth was always full of foreigners: people came there from every nation in the Empire, and few of them meant to stay long. Either they had come to make money by trading, or they were making money out of the traders. Some were criminals expelled from their own cities, or sailors looking for a ship, or refugees of some kind.

When people are far from home, or out to make money, they

often don't much care how they behave. There were constant riots in Corinth, and it wasn't safe to go out alone at night. Also, people with no home and no interest except money are apt to be very superstitious. "Luck" matters a lot to them, so Corinth was always full of peculiar religions, of people selling horoscopes or trying some new magic. Corinth had many temples, too, and the greatest of all crowned the steep rocky hill called the Acrocorinth, to the south of the city. This was the huge temple of Aphrodite, where a thousand slave girls served the goddess—Aphrodite was the goddess of sex, which is another reason why Corinth had quite a reputation.

This was the unlikely place in which Paul had decided to preach the good news of Jesus Christ.

HOW PAUL SET TO WORK

Paul walked through the crowded streets, looking carefully at what he saw, but he did not begin preaching immediately. He had his own way of setting about converting a new place. First he went to the Jewish quarter of the city. There were many Jews in Corinth, and they were quiet, respectable people, compared with some of the others. Paul was a Jew and he always went first to his own people, because they were the people God chose long ago, and from them the Savior, Christ, had come. So it was only right that the Jews should have the first chance to hear the good news that Christ brought.

Paul was a tentmaker by trade, and as he had no money, he wanted to work so that he wouldn't be a burden on anyone. He went to the street where the tentmakers lived. Jews are very hospitable people, and Paul was made welcome by a couple called Aquila and Priscilla, who were tentmakers. They had Roman names because they had lived in Rome. Just before our story begins, the Emperor Claudius had driven many Jews out of Rome and these two had come to Corinth. Paul learned a lot from them about Rome, as well as about Corinth. The three of them became firm friends.

On the Sabbath, Paul went to the synagogue—the Jewish meeting house for prayer. He preached the good news: that God had sent the promised Christ, and that he was Jesus of Nazareth, who died and rose again by the power of God, so that all those who believed in him might share his risen life. (He always spoke in the synagogues first, wherever he went, and so did the other apostles.) But, as usual, most of the Jews were very angry. They realized that the faith Paul preached was quite revolutionary. They believed that God had given them the Law, through Moses, and that as long as they kept the Law strictly they were doing God's will, they were all right with God. But Paul said that this old way was all over—only faith in Jesus was any good. Of course many of the Jews were furious.

But not all. Some realized that Paul was telling them something they had long been waiting to hear. They crowded round him and

Herbert G. May
The ruins of the marketplace of Athens where Paul argued for Christ.

asked for baptism. And Paul baptized them, among them the leader of the local synagogue, whose name was Crispus. So the Church at Corinth was founded, and as the news spread, it began to grow. All kinds of people heard the message that God was calling all men, however poor, however wicked, to change their lives and be a new people, through Jesus Christ.

Paul loved these people. He knew what they were like, he knew that many of them were weak and superstitious, self-indulgent and ignorant and vain. But they were sincere; they really believed in Jesus Christ; they really were changed by their faith, and were full of joy in the new life they had discovered. Paul knew they would need a lot of help, for their old life was so near—so near in their own past, and so near in the streets of the city, where others were living the kind of life the new Christians had only just left behind. Paul stayed in Corinth about two years, and that was a long time for a man as impatient as Paul. He preached to the unconverted, but he also taught the new Christians, the Church, and every week met with them to celebrate the Lord's Supper, when they shared bread and wine as a sign of the Lord's death.

This word "church," when you find it in the New Testament, doesn't mean a building. It means the people who were called together by Christ. Groups of them in various places were called, for example, "the Church at Corinth," or "the Church at Ephesus," or "the Church in Galatia." In Paul's time there were no special buildings for worship; the Church met in any house or hall that was big enough to celebrate the Lord's Supper.

The work of building up the Church in Corinth was not able to go on for long without troubles from the outside. You will remember that Paul had come to Corinth from Thessalonica, and now his companions, Timothy and Silas, arrived from there with news of trouble. It was because he received this news that Paul wrote his first letter, which we know as the First Letter to the Thessalonians.

Because Paul wrote this and his other letters, we, so many centuries later, are able still to hear his voice and listen to the way he preached the news of Jesus, which he called the good news. The work he began that day in Corinth is still going on, whenever we read or hear one of his epistles.

Portion of the marketplace of Corinth as seen from
the place of the tribunal.
Corinth was a major trading city in Paul's time.

TO KNOW PAUL BETTER

Make a map of the world which Paul knew, to help you remember the journeys he took. Fill in the map gradually as you read through this book.

The map should be big enough to put in detail without overcrowding. Use black pencil for place names and other colored pencils for Paul's travels, the Roman roads, sea routes, and so forth. Make a key for your map showing what the various colors mean.

You can begin by marking on the map the places mentioned in this chapter and the route Paul probably followed in traveling from Thessalonica to Athens and then to Corinth.

Read Acts of the Apostles, chapter 18, verses 1-3.

2 How Paul Wrote to Thessalonica_____

Timothy and Silas had traveled straight from the district of Thessalonica and Beroea, in Macedonia, and brought firsthand news of what was happening in the Church there. Their news caused Paul to send a letter to the Church in Thessalonica, and you will find this letter in your Bible, called 1 Thessalonians. (Although this is the first letter of Paul's that we have, it does not appear first in your Bible. His letters are usually arranged in order of length, the longest coming first.)

Paul didn't actually *write* his letters himself, though he usually wrote a little at the end, as a sort of signature, in his own handwriting. This was the usual thing to do. Except for short, personal notes, most letters were not written by the sender, but dictated to a secretary, or sometimes a public letter writer, who sat in the marketplace and would write anyone's letters for a small fee.

So Paul dictated his letters. But he didn't always dictate word for word what he wanted written down. He often did so, especially when he wanted to say something extra important or complicated, but sometimes he would simply tell the person who was acting as secretary the kind of thing he wanted to say and let him put it into the letter in his own way. This was quite usual—most people did it. And you mustn't think of Paul's secretaries as paid clerks, but rather as his friends and disciples, who shared his work and were good at writing. It wasn't as difficult as you might think for Paul's friends to write down his ideas, because they had heard him explain them so often to others. He wasn't dictating something quite new; usually he was simply explaining something they had often heard in his sermons and teaching.

Sometimes it seems as if Paul had left nearly all the work of composing the letter to his "secretary," for Paul was an impatient man. He was always in a hurry, because he knew that the whole world was hungry for the good news of Christ, and he was only one man, and there was so little time! After all, he never knew when he might be arrested and killed, or simply stabbed one dark night by one of his enemies, so he didn't want to spend a long time dictating. Sometimes we can almost see him, forced to break off some work of teaching and preaching because of news from one of the other Churches, and saying: "Oh—tell them this—and that—you know what to say! Let me get on with my work!" For although Paul loved all his converts he was the sort of man who gives his whole heart and attention to what he is doing *now*, and that was why he was such a marvelous preacher. Everyone who heard him knew that his whole self was in every word he said.

A QUESTION FROM THESSALONICA

But now, when Timothy arrived, although Paul was deeply concerned with the new Church at Corinth, he tore himself away from his work to welcome his friend. As he listened to Timothy's report, Paul remembered the faces of the people at Thessalonica; he remembered their joy at his preaching, their kindness, and their faith. Timothy told him that the Christians at Thessalonica were being persecuted (you will remember that Paul had to leave there in a hurry) but were bearing up well; and also that they were worried about something they did not understand.

In those days Christians thought that the world would soon come to an end. They knew that the triumph of the Lord Jesus was the beginning of a new age, so they felt that the present, wicked world must soon end altogether. They expected this to happen at any minute. The people in Thessalonica wanted to know if believers who died before the coming of the Lord Jesus would be able to share in his glory—or was his glory only for those who were still alive when he came? Paul had been the first to preach the faith to the Thessalonians; he felt responsible for them, and he knew that they would listen to his teaching on this matter. So he sent them a letter.

All letters at that time began with the names of the people who sent them, and Paul liked to include any other disciples who were with him when he wrote. So he began: "From Paul, Silvanus [another name for Silas], and Timothy, to the Church in Thessalonica which is in God the Father, and the Lord Jesus Christ: wishing you grace and peace."

To give them more confidence in their troubles Paul assured the

Thessalonians their faith and goodness were so well known that the news of it was helping people in other places to believe in the Lord Jesus. He told them how much he loved them, and trusted them, "like a mother caring for her children. We came to love you so much that we handed over to you not only the good news, but our own lives as well!"

He told them how much he would have liked to go back and visit them because, he says, "you are our pride and joy." But since he could not go himself he wanted Timothy to go, "who is God's helper in spreading the good news of Christ, to keep you firm and strong in the faith—and prevent any of you from being unsettled by the present troubles. But troubles were bound to come, we warned you to expect it. So I wanted to be sure about your faith. I was afraid the tempter might have tried you too hard."

Then Paul told them how glad he had been to hear Timothy's news of their steadfastness under persecution: "Your faith has been a great comfort to us in the middle of our own troubles and sorrows."

Above all, he told them to remember what kind of life they had

Herbert G. May
Ruins of the past in modern Thessalonica, a thriving city and port today, as in Paul's day

Herbert G. May
Excavations of the ancient marketplace in the modern city of Thessalonica

Don B. Parkinson
Today Christians gather to discuss Paul and his letters.
In much the same way, the Christians of Thessalonica gathered to hear Paul's
letters read and interpreted.

entered when they began to believe. It is the life God wants and "as you are already living it," a life of holiness, of unselfish love. Paul remembered with warm gratitude how the Thessalonians had welcomed and cared for him—no need to keep on telling *them* to love one another—"in fact this is what you are doing, with all the brothers throughout the whole of Macedonia," he wrote, "but go on making even greater progress."

THE END OF THE WORLD

As for the uncertainty in the minds of many believers about what Christ had meant by his promise to "come again," Paul reassured them. People have worried about this question on and off ever since those days. Sometimes they worry because they think the end of all things is about to come and they are afraid. Sometimes they worry because the coming seems so far off, they wonder what it can possibly mean, and whether Christ will ever come at all. In Paul's day there were many Jewish books and prophecies about the end of the world, and the Christians naturally talked about these things in a Jewish way. So Paul used the kind of words and images these books use, because that was how people were used to talking about the coming of God, the "day of the Lord." He spoke of God's "trumpet" sounding the end, and of the way human beings can meet God "in the air" or "in the clouds"—for people thought of God as being up "above" them.

But the important things that Paul told the Church at Thessalonica are as true for us as for them. He says: "We mustn't grieve for the dead, like people who have no hope. We believe that Jesus died and rose again, and that it will be the same for those who die in Jesus. It won't make any difference whether we have died already or are still alive. 'At the trumpet of God' those who have died in Christ, and those who are still alive will be taken up to meet the Lord 'in the air.' So we shall stay with the Lord for ever. Comfort one another with this. As for when this will happen—you don't really expect me to tell you that—you know it will come 'like a thief in the night,' just when it is least expected.

"But it won't catch *us* unawares, because we are not like people in the dark. We are 'sons of light,' we should be awake. To us the coming will not be a frightening punishment, it will be our salvation—it means that through Jesus Christ, who died for us, we shall be alive, with him. So give each other courage and strength, thinking of this!"

TO KNOW PAUL BETTER

To add to your knowledge of Paul and his friends, learn from the Acts of the Apostles the name of the place where Timothy came from, and also the name of Paul's hometown. Mark these on your map, and also mark other places mentioned in this chapter.

Find in the New Testament the First Letter to the Thessalonians.

3 The Day of the Lord

The Second Letter from Paul to the Church at Thessalonica is shorter than the first, but it is very like it. In fact, many of the things it says are almost exactly as in the first one. The big difference is that it points out several times that we don't know when "the day of the Lord" will come—it could be soon, but it may be a very long way ahead. And it repeats what the first letter had said—reminding the Church that Paul and his friends worked hard, so as not to be a burden to anyone, "so as to be an example." But this time the lesson is rubbed in much harder. What had happened, and why is this letter so much like the first and yet different in these ways?

Some people have thought that perhaps Paul didn't send this letter at all, but that someone else did so, *pretending* to be Paul. But this would seem a pointless thing to do, since so much of it is the same as the first one. Yet, if the letter really is from Paul, then why is there so much repetition? Perhaps we can get an idea of how this might have come about if we imagine all that was going on at the time.

PLOTS AND QUARRELS IN CORINTH

Paul was working all day and every day at building up the new Church at Corinth. He preached in the synagogue, and when he was driven out of the synagogue, he preached in the streets. Then, when people came to him individually, to learn more about Jesus Christ, he taught them and prepared them for baptism. But he didn't want everything in Corinth to depend on himself, so at the same time he was training some of the believers to be teachers, so that *they* could instruct the converts and baptize them, and encourage the new believers. He knew that he wouldn't be in Corinth for very long. At the same time, too, he was working as a tentmaker in order to earn his keep, because he always insisted on being independent—he didn't want anyone to think he was making money out of the gospel (though he also said that apostles and preachers did have a right to their keep).

24

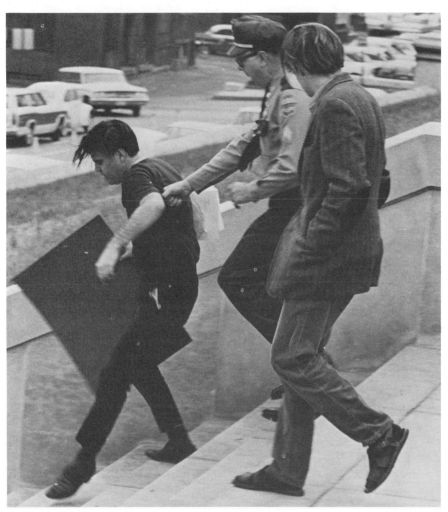

Richard T. Lee
Disagreement and sudden violence: a factor common to Paul's world and our own

As well as all this, there was the constant worry of threats from the furious Jews. Paul had to move out of the Jewish streets of the city. Instead, he went to lodge with a Roman called Titus, who had become a Christian and who lived near the synagogue. At one point the Jews were so angry at his preaching that they waited for Paul in the street and then dragged him in front of the Roman proconsul, Gallio. Gallio came from a distinguished Roman family. He was the brother of Seneca, a famous Roman writer. Like most Roman patricians (noblemen), Gallio thought the Jews were a rowdy, superstitious, primitive people, always making trouble. He was tired of their religious squabbles and refused to listen to their complaints. He told his lictors—his Roman bodyguard—to clear the court, and the pagan Corinthians, who had been listening, were delighted, because they too disliked the Jews and were glad to see them humiliated. Feeling that Gallio would be unlikely to interfere, they decided to make the most of their chance. So they seized Sosthenes, the new leader of the synagogue, and beat him —right in front of the seat of justice. But, as Luke says in the Acts of the apostles, Gallio took no notice of all this.

After this, the Jews showed their hostility less. But you can see the kind of atmosphere in which Paul had to work—plots and quarrels and feuds all around him, and he was trying to preach the gospel of peace and love! Sometimes he must have been near despair, at other times he was angry—the Corinthians often made him angry—and he needed all his faith to help him. Sometimes he wondered if he wasn't making the situation worse, because his preaching aroused such anger. And, for all his great courage, the constant threats to his life got him down, too. We can see how deeply worried he was from a dream he told his friend Luke, who wrote it down in Acts. In the dream, the Lord said to Paul: "Don't be afraid, but speak, and do not be silent. For I am with you and no one shall attack you or harm you, for I have many people in this city."

WHY SHOULD CHRISTIANS HAVE TO WORK?

It was in the middle of all this that messengers came again from Thessalonica. They reported that Paul's last letter had cheered the Church there, and they were full of gladness at the thought of being with Jesus forever. But some of them were so excited about this that in spite of what Paul had said about the uncertainty of the time, they felt sure the Lord would come very soon. In that case, why bother to work? The messengers said that these people were "living in idleness, doing no work themselves and interfering with everyone else's."

No wonder Paul was exasperated. He realized something would have to be done—such a way of living was not at all the way of holiness and love, it was irresponsible and selfish—and yet they *were* good people, they really did believe and want to follow the way of Jesus! We can imagine him saying to a friend—perhaps it was Timothy: "Why haven't they understood? I thought I said it quite clearly! For goodness' sake write and tell them that's not the way to behave. Tell them what I said before—only more so. But you'd better explain as clearly as possible that we've no reason to suppose the day of the Lord is just around the corner. I told them when I was there—the prophecies tell of all kinds of things that are bound to happen before the end. They've all heard about it often enough, but remind them. Tell them we *order* the lazy ones to go on quietly with their work and *earn* the food they eat! As I do! And tell them that anyone who doesn't obey should be made to feel he's in the wrong—he shouldn't be welcomed. But don't let them treat him as an enemy; he's their brother, but he needs correcting."

So the letter was written. There is a lot in it about the things that are to happen before the day of the Lord comes. The people who heard the letter read knew all about this; we don't, so we can only guess what is meant by some of the things it refers to: for example, by "the rebel" who is to appear before the end, and do signs and wonders, and deceive many people. But the really important part repeats and strengthens what Paul had said in his first letter.

WHAT MATTERS IS FAITH

Whether Paul dictated this second letter to the Thessalonians or whether the writer was simply putting down what he thought was most important in Paul's message makes little difference. The letter insists that what matters is faith: faith comes to us not out of our own heads, not from dreams or visions, but from the word of the gospel, and this is brought to us by someone else who has faith, who in turn learned from another—and so on, back to where our faith begins, back to the very source of our faith, Jesus. This is the *tradition,* which means "handing on." What is handed on, whether by word of mouth or by letter, is the good news—the gospel. The good news is not just *facts about* Jesus Christ, it is a new *life*, a life which is the glory of our Lord Jesus Christ, and we come to this life by *faith*. Faith doesn't mean just believing a fact, it means being called by God and answering his call. The letter tries to explain this as it says: "God chose you among his first ones, to be saved by the spirit that makes us holy, and by *faith* in the truth. Through the good news that we brought he called you to this, so that you should share the glory of our Lord Jesus Christ."

When Paul dictated this letter to Thessalonica (or ordered a letter to be sent) he was only just beginning to work out his ideas

Israel Office of Information

Remains of ancient synagogue near the Sea of Galilee. In the many cities where Paul taught he always went to the synagogue first.

about faith and calling. Later he explained what he meant more clearly. But at this time, when he had to interrupt his work in Corinth to help the Church at Thessalonica, we can see him grappling with difficult, new ideas. When we read his letters now, we sometimes feel as if Paul knew all the answers already. But it is a help if we see that he didn't know all the answers. People kept on asking him new questions, confronting him with new problems. He had no stock answers. He knew only one thing for certain— that Jesus Christ has risen from the dead by the power of God, and that he, Paul, had seen him. All the rest he worked out.

But he didn't do it in isolation. The *Church* was working it out. Not by sitting down and studying, but by *living,* seeing, questioning, and sometimes arguing, and also by praying and loving. The Church that had begun in the upper room at Pentecost about twenty years earlier was already many thousands strong, but it was still very new. It was tackling problems no one had ever dreamed of before. It needed new minds, speaking a new language, fit for a new life in a new world. And so there was Paul, who couldn't think a secondhand thought if he tried. He gave the Church a new language, which it has used ever since.

TO KNOW PAUL BETTER

To understand more about Paul's background and his work, find out what a Jewish synagogue looked like, and draw it. Find out why the Jews had synagogues. What is the difference between a synagogue and a church?

Learn what Old English words our modern word "gospel" comes from.

Read the Second Letter to the Thessalonians.

4 "Are You Mad, Galatians?"

After nearly two years Paul left Corinth and took passage on a ship sailing east. He took with him his friends, the two Roman Jews, Aquila and his wife Priscilla, because they were very good at teaching converts and he needed them to help him. This journey (see map, page 12) was probably made in the summer of A.D. 52.

They sailed to Ephesus, a big port which was famous for its huge temple of Artemis, the goddess of fertility. (Her Roman name is Diana.) As usual, Paul preached in the synagogue there, and he impressed people very much. But he would not stay long—he wanted to reach Jerusalem, where he could talk over his work with some of the other apostles. He had a great deal to tell them, as well as to hear.

A MEETING OF THE APOSTLES IN JERUSALEM

It was necessary, too, for the apostles to decide a very important question: Could people who were not Jews be baptized as followers of Christ? All the first apostles were Jews. The Jewish Law demanded circumcision and the following of innumerable regulations that governed every aspect of daily life. Many of the Jewish Christians thought that this was an essential part of Christianity, and that only Jews could be truly Christian; or, at least, that those non-Jews (Gentiles) who were baptized must also be circumcised and follow the Jewish Law. Paul did not agree with this. He was sure that Jesus wanted the good news preached to all men, whether Jew or Gentile.

This matter was discussed by all the apostles, and it was agreed that it was not necessary for Gentile converts to accept the Jewish Law. It was enough for them to follow the law of Christ.

After his meeting in Jerusalem with the other apostles, Paul went north again, visiting Antioch in Syria, where the first mainly Gentile Church had been founded. (It was in Antioch that the followers of Jesus Christ were given the nickname "Christian," and the name stuck!)

From Antioch, Paul went on, preaching in the districts of Asia Minor called Galatia and Phrygia. He had been there before, and there were already Churches in several big cities there. The believers in all the places he visited welcomed him enthusiastically, but he didn't stay more than a few months in any one place. (His return journey from Antioch is shown in the map on page 36.)

G. Eric Matson
View of Jerusalem from the south. Paul could have traveled a road like this one on his way to the meeting of the Apostles in Jerusalem.

He wanted to return to Ephesus and use it as his base, even if he had to make frequent journeys out from there. Ephesus, like Corinth, was a huge trading center. There were regular passenger and freight services by sea, especially to and from Rome, Corinth, and Caesarea (the port of Jerusalem). One of the main Roman roads, the Egnation Way, led from Ephesus to the chief inland cities of Asia Minor. For all these reasons, Ephesus was very suitable for Paul's purposes. He could preach to the people who lived in the city itself, and also to those who passed through it. He could be sure of getting the latest news of the Churches in Asia Minor, and also from the mother Church at Jerusalem, and from Corinth and Macedonia.

Yet, despite his hurry, Paul's travels took a long time, and it was not until A.D. 54 that he came back to Ephesus. He had not been there long before news did reach him, from the Churches of the district of Galatia. The news was bad. It told of trouble, between Jewish Christians and Gentile Christians, of exactly the kind that Paul had feared when he had gone to Jerusalem to discuss the matter with the other apostles. This was not the first time Paul had met this kind of conflict, and it was not to be the last.

THE GALATIANS QUESTION PAUL'S AUTHORITY

For no sooner had Paul left Galatia than certain Jewish teachers began to undo his work. "Who does Paul think he is?" they said. "What right has he to preach? He never saw Jesus, as the other apostles did. Paul was not sent by Jesus," they said, "he is simply working under the orders of the twelve who are the real apostles. *They* never said the old Jewish Law was finished. It is only Paul who preaches this dangerous doctrine. Foreigners can only be saved if they obey the Law and are circumcised!" The people who taught this claimed to be speaking on behalf of the apostles: they said they had come from Jerusalem, the mother Church of all believers, the one Jesus himself had founded. So it is no wonder that the believers in Galatia were upset, and began to think that Paul had been wrong. Trouble and argument followed, and peace was destroyed.

When he learned of this, Paul wrote to the Galatians. This letter sounds as if it had been dictated in bits and pieces and in a hurry.

Herbert G. May
City gateway at Jerusalem excavated in 1966, below the level of the present
Damascus gate. It was built by Herod Agrippa I (A.D. 41-44) shortly before
Paul's first visit to Corinth.

Paul was trying to sort out the problem of preaching in Ephesus, and at the same time to think of a way of convincing the Galatian Churches that he really was a true apostle and that, since they were Gentiles, they were truly free from the Law. It was a difficult thing to explain, because he didn't want to give the impression that the Law was bad or useless. Yet it was so important that these people who had been given the freedom of faith should not be tied up again in the endless detailed rules of the Law of Moses.

So this letter is angry and affectionate, full of strong arguments and very downright sayings; in it you can feel Paul's love for his converts and yet his exasperation with their feebleness, and his rage against the people who misled *them* and slandered *him*.

It is also interesting because it gives a short account of Paul's own life after his conversion.

"It didn't take you long to turn away from the one who called you," he said.

"You've chosen a 'different' good news—but there is only *one* good news which I preached to you. It isn't a human message. I wasn't given it by men. I learned it straight from Jesus Christ. You must have heard how I, as a Jew, persecuted the Church of God, how enthusiastic I was for the old traditions of my people! But God had chosen me, even before I was born, to preach the good news to the pagans. He revealed his Son to me!"

Paul explained that he had scarcely met the other apostles for many years, so he couldn't have learned his ideas from them. And when he did get to know them, they approved his teaching, realizing that he had been especially chosen to preach to other nations. Titus, who was a Greek boy and had come to Jerusalem with Paul, was not circumcised, although some of the Jerusalem Christians said he ought to be, according to the Law.

"Then James and Cephas and John, the leaders, shook hands with Barnabas and me as a sign of partnership. We were to go to the pagans and they to the circumcised (the Jews)."

And later, when even Peter had to give in to those who said all Christians should keep the Jewish Law, "I stood up to him and opposed him to his face, because he was clearly in the wrong.

"For what makes man right with God is not obedience to the Law, but *faith* in Jesus. No one can do God's will by keeping the

Law. It's as if I'd been crucified with Christ—so now I don't live my own life, my only life is the life that Christ lives *in* me. And the life I now live is a life of *faith*. But if the *Law* can make us right with God, what was the point of Christ's death?

Herbert G. May
The harbor at Caesarea on the coast of Israel, to which Paul returned from two missionary journeys and from which he sailed to Rome.
It had been built by Herod the Great.

"Are you people in Galatia mad, or bewitched? I'll ask you one question—did you receive the Spirit of God because you kept the Law, or because you *believed* what was preached to you?"

He reminded them that Abraham, who lived long before the

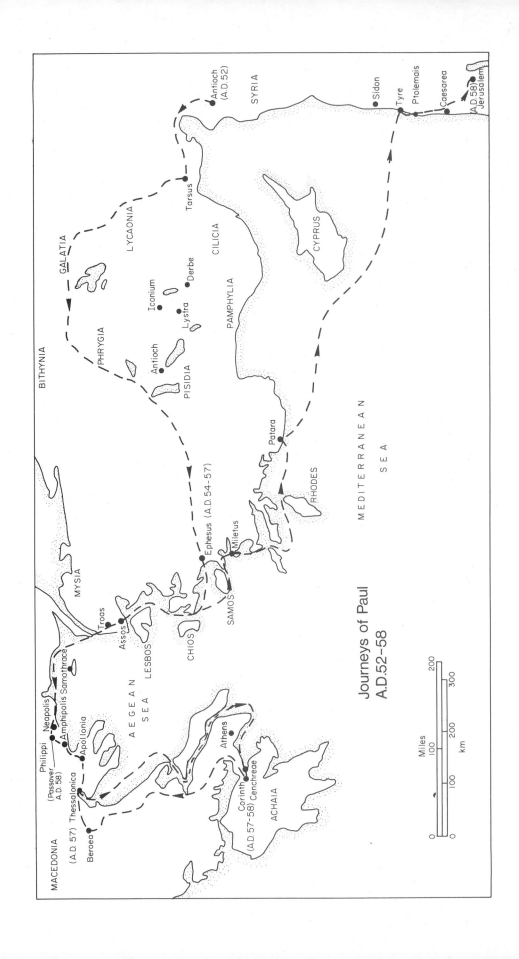

Journeys of Paul
A.D. 52–58

Law was given, was made holy because he had *faith*. But, the Galatians might ask, in that case why did God ever give the Law? Paul explained that the Law was given so that people would understand what was wrong, and realize they were not free, could do nothing for themselves, for sin was everywhere, however hard they tried to avoid it. But God promised that he would save his people from this slavery, and he kept his promise—Christ has set us free. The Christian lives by the Spirit, not by the Law.

"When Christ freed us, he meant us to *stay* free! Stand firm, then, and don't allow yourselves to be made slaves again.

"But if you are called to freedom, do not make that an excuse for giving in to selfish desires and feelings. Care for each other, with *love*, for after all the whole Law is summed up in this commandment: 'Love your neighbor as yourself.' The life of the Spirit is a life of love, and makes you happy. You can't belong to Christ unless you 'crucify' all selfish desires and feelings. But it doesn't matter whether you are circumcised or not—what matters is that you are a *new creation*, the Israel of God."

TO KNOW PAUL BETTER

To help you understand the young Church and its beginnings learn the names of the twelve apostles and write them down. Beside each name, write down the apostle's occupation before he was called by Jesus.

Read Acts of the Apostles, chapter 15, verses 5-29, which tell of the meeting in Jerusalem, what decision was made at the meeting and for what reason.

Mark on your map the places mentioned in this chapter and the routes traveled by Paul.

5 Bad News from Corinth _____

Paul spent three years in Ephesus, and he found plenty to do there. But he was not allowed to continue his preaching in peace. People kept arriving with requests for help, with complaints or questions, from all the Churches. When he could, he sent messages by word of mouth; sometimes he sent one of his helpers, as his representative, to try to sort things out. But sometimes there was nothing to do but to drop everything and send a letter.

Only a few of Paul's letters have been preserved. We know of a few others he did send because he mentions them in the ones we have, but there may have been more, especially shorter ones. All the same, Paul wasn't by nature a writer. This may surprise you. Nearly all we know about him comes to us from his letters (and from the account of his adventures in the Acts of the Apostles) and it is easy to think of him pen in hand, a quiet, reflective man. But when you read his letters you can see that this idea is wrong. Paul was first of all a preacher: he liked to meet people face to face and tell them the good news, so that they would almost *catch* the faith from him.

When he had to write (or rather, dictate) it was only to clear up a misunderstanding or explain a difficult idea. Paul would never have dreamed of using letters to preach the gospel—that *must* be done by people to other people, face to face.

But we can be thankful that Paul was often obliged to put his ideas into writing, because otherwise we would have very little idea of what his preaching was like. For instance, we can tell the kind of ideas he had used when preaching to the Corinthians from the letter he wrote to them later, when they had got into a mess. And this they certainly did.

APOLLOS SENDS PAUL A MESSAGE

Sometime about A.D. 57, when Paul had already been at Ephesus for a couple of years, disturbing news reached him from Corinth.

38

We don't know for certain who brought the letter containing the news; it may have been Erastus, a Greek convert. Whoever the messenger was, it seems possible that the person who sent the news was a man called Apollos. Apollos was a Jew from Alexandria, who had come to Ephesus just after Paul left there the first time. He had been baptized by John the Baptist, but he had heard of the teaching of Jesus, and believed it, though he hadn't joined a group of believers and so didn't yet belong to a Church. He came to Ephesus to preach about Jesus to the Jews there. Paul's friends, Aquila and Priscilla, heard him and explained to him the things he hadn't yet learned about the way of Jesus. So Apollos joined the Church, and soon afterward he left for Greece, to help spread the gospel. He went to Corinth, and was a great help there because he was a Jew and very learned. So he was able to speak with the Jews there, showing them from scripture that Jesus was the Christ. Soon Apollos had a great many followers.

Now Apollos realized that some of the Corinthian Christians were not living up to their calling as children of God. They were slipping back into the old pagan ways of living, and quarreling and arguing among themselves. When Paul had been there, he had sorted everything out, but now he was gone, and although he had promised to come back it had been a long time and he had not returned. They were wondering whether he ever would come, and they were forgetting some of his teaching, or feeling it was all too difficult. This was the news that reached Paul at Ephesus. No wonder he was worried by it; it looked as if much of his work was being undone.

Paul's first idea was to go to Corinth himself, but the state of affairs in Ephesus made that impossible. More and more people were asking about the new faith, and of course there was the usual trouble with some of the Jews because they were so obstinate in refusing to listen to him, and prevented others from listening. Paul stopped preaching in the synagogue and started giving lectures every day in a public hall, where many more people could listen to him. Hundreds came to hear him, but not all were friendly. So, what with all the converts to be taught and enemies to be argued with, Paul could not leave Ephesus. Too much depended on him —his job was very much a one-man show. Although he always

Nash, from Three Lions
Rome, the Church of Santa Prisca founded in A.D. 280 on the traditional site
of the house of Aquila and Priscilla, two Christians who moved to Corinth
and welcomed Paul there.

tried to train others to carry on his work, this took a long time. Meanwhile, he could not go away.

A LETTER TO THE CORINTHIANS

Instead, he sent Timothy and Erastus, who was a Corinthian himself (he may have been the one who brought the news). Paul sent a letter with them, but this letter is lost, though it is mentioned in a later one. (It seems possible, though, that parts of this lost letter were put together with another, later letter, the one we call Second Corinthians. Parts of Second Corinthians are certainly not in the places they were written for, and as they deal with the sort of thing Paul said he had written in that first letter, they may have come from it. These parts are chapter 9, and chapter 6, verse 14 to chapter 7, verse 1, in 2 Corinthians. Look them up and see what you think.)

In this first letter Paul told the Corinthian believers to keep away from immoral people who drag them back to paganism. But Timothy was to deliver most of his message personally: he was to remind the Church how a believer ought to live the way of Jesus, just as Paul had taught it to all his converts, and as he lived it himself, in Christ. Paul was never afraid to point to himself as an example, because he was so certain that all the power he possessed was the power of the Spirit. He knew he could do nothing alone—he was physically small, not very strong, and if he was really excited when he preached, he was apt to get tied up in his own sentences. But his own lack of dignity or wisdom made it all the clearer that he was using a power greater than his own, a power which filled his whole being. That was what made people listen, and that was why he often said "look at me" or "do as I do"—because he was what Christ had made him, and Christ could do as much for others, if only they would let him.

So Timothy and Erastus went to Corinth, but the situation there was too difficult for them to cope with. The Church was split into groups, all arguing, and all thinking they were right and the rest wrong. And they were so busy quarreling that they were forgetting to pray, forgetting even the reason for their quarrels, and easily taking up again the pagan life they had left. Everyone had a grievance, and nobody wanted to listen to anyone else. The only

Herbert G. May
The paved road at Ephesus leading from the harbor to the theater. Paul spent much time in this ancient city.

thing they had agreed about was that Paul himself must come and settle it. At last it was decided to send a special delegation to Paul to ask his advice, and if possible to get him to come in person.

Herbert G. May
The theater at Ephesus, the city where the silversmiths stirred
up a riot against the Christians

TO KNOW PAUL BETTER

*To learn more about one of the places where Paul established
a church, read about the city of Corinth. At one time Corinth was
destroyed. A Roman emperor ordered it to be rebuilt. When was it
destroyed and why, and which emperor ordered its rebuilding?*

*The map you have made should show all the places mentioned
so far and the routes by which Paul traveled.*

*This book began with Paul's journey from Thessalonica to
Corinth, in A.D. 50. This was not the first journey Paul had made.
Look up the route of what is known as Paul's "first missionary journey," made from A.D. 45 through A.D. 49, and, using a different
color, mark it on your map. Name the places he visited.*

6 The Foolish Corinthians

in Corinth arrived in Ephesus. Among them was Apollos himself; Stephanas, whose family had been among the first of Paul's converts in Greece—he had left his family behind in order to come; and Fortunatus and Achaicus, who were probably from the household of a rich Corinthian lady called Chloe.

They had a sad tale to tell, and Apollos felt that he himself had been the cause of some of the trouble, without meaning to be. He had been teaching and preaching in Corinth, and he did it in his own way. And, of course, his way was not the same as Paul's since he was a different kind of person. Some of the Corinthian believers liked his way better than Paul's, and said so, and even called themselves "Apollos' party." Others said, "No, Paul is better, I'm for Paul." Still others knew that Cephas (another name for the apostle Peter) was the chief of the apostles, so they said, "I'm for Cephas." But some of them thought they would go one better. "I'm for Christ," they said, and they would not listen to any teachers at all. And so divisions and quarreling arose.

Each of these "parties" was sure it knew all the answers. They argued endlessly, using bits of Greek philosophy to show how clever they were. Besides all this, many of the believers were behaving in immoral ways, living like pagans, and getting drunk— even when they celebrated the Lord's Supper. They were excited about the visions and gifts that came to some believers—but in the middle of all the quarreling and bad behavior none of these gifts really helped to make people holy. It was all a long way from the new life in Christ that Paul had tried to show them.

So Paul dictated his first long letter to Corinth, the one you will find in your Bible as 1 Corinthians. It was one of the longest he ever sent.

WHOSE SIDE ARE YOU ON?

Paul addressed the people at Corinth as "the holy people of Jesus Christ," in spite of their behavior, for it was the holiness to which they were called that showed up the wrongness of their behavior. To belong to Christ they must be united, not split into parties.

"What are all these slogans you have, like 'I am for Paul,' 'I am for Apollos,' 'I am for Cephas,' 'I am for Christ'? Has Christ been parceled out? Was it Paul that was crucified for you? Were you baptized in the name of Paul?

"But in fact my main work is not to baptize but to preach the good news—and all this clever philosophy is no use for that, you can't talk about the cross of Christ in that way. It is not the language of the philosophers, but of God's power to save. We can't be saved by human wisdom, but God's wisdom has made human cleverness look silly. He saves us by the faith that comes from the 'foolishness' of our message. The Jews want wonders and signs to prove God's power to them, and the Greeks want everything set out in neat arguments. We preach Christ crucified, and to the Jews that seems an obstacle they can't get over, while to the Greeks it seems simply crazy. But to those who have been called (whether they are Jews or Greeks) it is Christ who is the power of God and the wisdom of God. For God's foolishness is wiser than man's cleverness, and God's weakness is stronger than human strength."

Paul thought of the people among whom he had lived and taught in Corinth, not rich or educated or respectable people. Not at all the kind of people one would imagine were likely to become holy. They certainly had nothing to boast of. But it is the ones the world thinks common and contemptible that God has chosen—those who are nothing at all, to show up those who are everything.

"And I myself didn't impress you with my wisdom and my power of making speeches. I simply told you what God has shown me—my only knowledge was Jesus—the crucified Christ. Your faith doesn't depend on human wisdom, but on God's power. A man who has this Spirit can understand, because the Spirit reaches the depths of everything. But as for you—I didn't treat *you* as spiritual men, you were more like *babies* in Christ, you had to have milk, you weren't ready for solid food—and you still aren't! You are still not living by the Spirit—your slogans show this—'I am for Paul,' 'I am for Apollos.' What is Apollos and what is Paul? They are both servants, who brought the faith to you."

Athens, on the hill of the Areopagus where the council met.
The Acropolis is in the background. Stephanas was from the family
which had been among the first of Paul's converts in Greece.

As Paul thought of all that he had tried to do, and that Apollos
had tried to do after him, he became angrier and angrier. Paul in
a rage was not a person one would want to meet—he could be
fiercely sarcastic sometimes. Yet he loved these Corinthians, and
that was why their vanity and boasting made him so angry. They
could do so much if only they would let God work in them.

"We apostles are fools for Christ's sake—you are learned men, of course! We have no power—you have influence, you are famous! While we are nobodies! I'm saying all this to bring you to your senses, my dearest children—for I became your father in Christ Jesus when I preached the good news to you. That was why I sent Timothy, when I could not come myself. But I am coming soon—and whether I come with a stick or a loving greeting depends on you!"

BE HOLY

With this warning Paul went on to make it clear that sexual immorality was quite out of keeping with holiness. This may seem obvious to us—but it wasn't at all obvious in a city like Corinth, where sexual license was taken for granted, and Aphrodite, the goddess of sex, was worshiped with abandon. Paul explained that sexual self-indulgence is wrong because the human body is good and is meant to be holy. It is meant for love, in marriage, so husbands and wives should love each other and be faithful to each other. But some—like Paul himself—should stay unmarried, in order to be able to work to spread the gospel without worrying about a family.

Another matter troubling the Corinthians was whether a Christian might buy the meat of animals that had been offered in sacrifice in the pagan temples. This meat was offered for sale in the markets, once the ceremonies were over. Paul had a commonsense answer to this problem: "As for sacrificed meat, it's really just like any other meat—but don't eat it if it makes people think you are joining in pagan practices."

He warned them, too, to be careful to celebrate the Lord's Supper with reverence: the Corinthians were accustomed to having a community feast before celebrating the Lord's Supper, and on occasion, the richer of them were greedy or got drunk, while the poorer ones went hungry. Paul reminded them that to behave like this is to insult the Lord. "Anyone who eats the bread or drinks the cup unworthily will be behaving unworthily toward the body and blood of the Lord."

The most important message that Paul had to give to the Church at Corinth was about what *kind* of life it was to which they were called. He had often told them it was a life in the Spirit, but how did this show itself? What kinds of behavior, what "gifts," showed that the Spirit of Christ was truly at work? The Corinthians were impressed by extraordinary gifts that came to some people, enabling them to speak strange languages, to heal people, or to prophesy.

"Yes, all these come from God, but they are not necessarily the most important. There are many gifts and they all come from the same Spirit, just as the body has many parts, yet is one body. But not all the parts are equally important. You are all Christ's body, but each is a different part of it. . . . First there are apostles, then prophets, then teachers, then the gift of miracles, and healing, giving money generously, and so on. But there is another way that is best of all. . . ."

Then Paul went on to dictate the passage which has become among the most famous of all Christian writings: 1 Corinthians, chapter 13: the praise of *love*, which is truly the best gift of the Spirit. When all else fails, there are three things that last—faith, hope, and love, and the greatest of these is love.

CAN THE DEAD RISE?

There was one last question that Paul had to deal with, and it was rather like the one he had written about to Thessalonica. The Greeks thought of the human body and soul as two separate things, the soul dwelling in the body and leaving it at death. But Paul was a Jew, and Jews always thought of human beings as one whole. "If we are all to share in the life of the risen Jesus, what about our bodies?" they asked. "How can dead bodies live? Is there really a resurrection?"

Paul tried to explain the resurrection by talking of a seed, which is planted in the ground and grows into something that seems quite different, yet is the same plant. "It is sown a physical body, it is raised a spiritual body." What is important is not his explanation, because this is something that cannot be fully explained. What is important is that the resurrection is something that *will happen*.

"I preach what all the apostles preach, that Jesus Christ died for your sins, was buried, and rose on the third day. He appeared to many witnesses, and last of all to me, also. This is what you all

Herbert G. May
The marketplace of Corinth, where Paul stayed for a year and
a half. A delegation from this city went to Ephesus to meet
with Paul and discuss the problems of the church at Corinth.

believed. If Christ is not risen then your believing is useless, we are
shown up as lying witnesses. But Christ *has* in fact been raised
from the dead, he is the firstfruits of the dead. Just as all men die,
in Adam, so all men will be brought to life, in Christ."

Can't they realize? Paul seems to be saying—here I am, wearing
myself out, struggling to get people to understand—what do they

think I'm getting out of it? I might be killed any day by furious people who behave more like animals than men. Why should I do all this if the end of it is nothing but death?

"I face death every day, brothers—if my hope was only a human hope, why should I have to struggle with these wild beasts at Ephesus?

"Now let us thank God, for making us sure of victory through our Lord Jesus Christ."

TO KNOW PAUL BETTER

Paul worked with people of several different countries who spoke many different languages. "Cephas" and "Peter" are two words from different languages which have the same meaning. Which language does each word come from? What is the meaning?

Peter had yet another name. What was it?

Look up and read the ending of the First Letter to the Corinthians, chapter 16, verses 21-24.

7 In Chains for Christ

Paul's life was a dangerous one. As he says in a letter to the Corinthians, "I have worked harder [than others]. I have been sent to prison more often, and been whipped so many times more, often almost to death."

It seems likely that he was in prison in Ephesus, though not for very long. We have no direct evidence of this (for example, it is not mentioned in the Acts of the Apostles), but Paul's letter to the Church at Philippi, which was probably written at about this time (A.D. 56–57), indicates that he is writing from prison. (You will find it in your Bible, called Letter to the Philippians.)

We do not know what accusation would have sent Paul to prison, but we do know that at the time he wrote this letter he had not yet been tried, and he was fairly certain that he would be set free once his trial had been held. It wasn't the first time his enemies had had him arrested on a trumped-up charge, and the Roman authorities didn't take Jewish accusations very seriously. Since he had been accused, they had to try him, of course, for the sake of justice—the Romans had a great respect for justice—but even before the trial they must have known Paul was innocent, and so he was well treated.

As a rule, there were no special prison buildings in the ancient world, and the cells were usually in the governor's house, the praetorium. This is where Paul was held. He was allowed to see his friends, to send letters and receive presents. And he certainly didn't let his imprisonment stop his work—he even turned it to advantage.

"I'm glad to tell you, brothers, that the things that have happened to me have actually been a help to the good news. My chains [he means his imprisonment, it's unlikely he was actually chained] for Christ's sake have become famous not only all over the praetorium [the governor's house] but in other places, too, and most of the brothers have become even braver because of these chains of mine. They are more and more daring in announcing the message."

Herbert G. May

A late local tradition at Philippi places Paul's prison at Philippi here in the crypt to the right of the steps

A LETTER TO THE CHURCH IN PHILIPPI

There were several reasons why Paul wanted to write to the Christians in Philippi. Philippi, like Ephesus, was a Roman colony, and one of the largest cities in Macedonia. Paul was very fond of his converts there. On his second missionary journey, when Silas was with him, it was the first place he had come to. He had founded the Church there, and he had been beaten and imprisoned there, too. He had suffered very much in order to found this Church, and he loved it especially.

Now that he was in prison, he had the time to send a newsy, friendly letter to the community he was so fond of.

The Philippians, too, were having trouble with the same people

52

who were worrying the Galatians, who were insisting that all Christians should be circumcised and keep the Law of Moses. There was disagreement and quarreling among the Philippians themselves, as well.

The letter in your Bible that is called Letter to the Philippians may even be made up from bits of several different letters which were put together at a later date.

In one place he says, "It's no trouble to repeat what I wrote to you before—just to be on the safe side. Look out for the mischief-makers! Watch out for the 'cutters' [he meant the people who wanted to circumcise all Christians]. *We* are the real people of the circumcision; because we worship according to the Spirit of God, we don't depend on an operation on our bodies! After all, I'm a Jew, I was circumcised when I was eight days old. As far as the Law *can* make you perfect, I was faultless! But because of Christ I now know that these 'advantages' are really *dis*advantages. I look on everything else as so much rubbish if only I can have Christ. All I want to know is Christ, and the power of his resurrection, and to share his suffering, following out in myself the pattern of his death."

But Paul didn't want anyone to think that because they belonged to Christ they could stop trying, and become holy without any effort. He explained this by talking about life as a race to be won. "I'm far from thinking I've already won! I forget the past and strain ahead. I am racing for the finish, for the 'prize' to which God calls us."

He begged them to be one, in love, and he reminded them to beware of the people who would divide them, of Jews who cared more for the rules about food and about circumcision of the body, than for the things that are important for the *whole* human life, forever—the things of the Spirit. "They make food [the laws about eating] into a kind of god, and they are proud of what is least important."

There is a lot of news and greetings to friends in the Letter to the Philippians. Paul talks about Timothy, whom he means to send to Philippi soon, so that he can bring back news. "I have nobody else like him!" Paul states. And he is going to send back Epaphroditus, who had come with messages from Philippi but had been ill and unable to go back before. "Give him a hearty welcome in the Lord, people like this deserve to be honored." But Paul, who could admire and praise so generously, couldn't stand people who didn't give their very best. "All the rest seem more interested in themselves than in Jesus Christ," he says sweepingly, though it is surely difficult to believe that *no one* but Timothy and Epaphroditus "cared for Christ."

Paul must have been a difficult man to work with, because he would never accept anything less than *all* as good enough for Christ. But also he saw in his own mind so clearly what should be done that he was unwilling to listen to anyone else's ideas, and was inclined to call people selfish or disloyal when they didn't do things *his* way. He certainly managed to disagree violently with some very good and experienced men, like Barnabas, for instance. Yet, with the weak and sinful he could be very, very gentle and patient. It was his helpers whom he drove so hard, as he drove himself, for the sake of the millions who were waiting for the message of Christ.

Herbert G. May
The marketplace at Philippi, a Roman colony and one of the largest cities of Macedonia during the time Paul taught there.

A HYMN TO CHRIST

The most famous passage in the letter to Philippi is a hymn. It was probably one that Christians sang in their assemblies for worship, and it may not have been written by Paul at all. It is a beautiful hymn, and very interesting because it shows us how these first Christians thought about Christ, their Lord. Paul quotes this hymn because he had been talking about the need for love and humility. And he begins by talking about what we now call the "Trinity," though nobody used that word then.

"If our life in Christ means anything to you, if Love [he means the Father, who is Love] can persuade you, or the Spirit that we share—then be one in believing and in love and in purpose. That's the one thing that would make me happy! There should be no conceit, no competing. Nobody should think of himself first, but of others instead. In your minds you must be the same as Christ Jesus."

Then he quotes the hymn:

"He was divine.
Yet he did not cling
to being equal with God,
but emptied himself,
and took on the state of a servant
and became a man like other men,
yet he became even humbler,
even to the point of accepting death—
death on a cross.
But God raised him high
and gave him a Name
which is above all other names
so that all beings
in the heaven, on earth, and under the earth,
should bend the knee at the name of Jesus,
and that every tongue should praise
Jesus Christ as Lord,
to the Glory of God the Father."

Paul often found himself in difficult situations, having to work under trying circumstances. Search for a description of prisons during Paul's times. Were they like those of the present day? How did Rome treat prisoners such as Paul?

Schalek, from Three Lions
Remnants of a basilica in the ruins of Philippi. Paul founded the first European Christian community in Philippi.

8 Earthenware Jars

"We are only the earthenware jars that hold this treasure, to make it clear that this huge power comes from God and not from us."

This image comes from Paul, writing again to Corinth in the letter we call 2 Corinthians, and the treasure he is talking about is the faith which he preached. This letter was perhaps written in A.D. 57, and about this time he must have wondered whether the earthenware jar (himself) might soon crack, as it was getting such rough use.

Paul was still in Ephesus, and when he was not in prison, or settling matters with the local authorities to avoid being imprisoned again, he worked at his daily preaching in the lecture hall, and at building up a strong and faithful Church in Ephesus. He impressed even the pagans, and some priests of Artemis respected and admired him so much that they were willing to protect him from his enemies.

But before long fresh news came from Corinth, and it was not good news. The quarrels and arguments which his first letter had been designed to end were just as bad, and there were some who were ready to say, as the false teachers in Galatia had said, that Paul was no true apostle, but an upstart, an ambitious man who wanted to make himself important! Paul was bitterly hurt; he had taken so much trouble not to be an expense to anyone in Corinth, and now they said he was exploiting the people for his own ends, that his message was false. He was angry not because of this insult to himself, but because if the Corinthians learned to despise him they would also despise his teaching, and that teaching was God's message and their salvation.

He sent Timothy to Corinth again, to try to settle matters, but Timothy met only insults, and returned to report to Paul. Paul realized there was nothing to do but to go there himself, although he knew that his absence would give his enemies in Ephesus the chance they had been waiting for. So Paul sailed for Corinth, hoping to reconcile the disputing parties and restore the peace of the gospel. Instead he was met by defiance, and one man in particular aroused many of the people to refuse obedience to Paul. Given time, Paul might have succeeded in winning back those of his converts who had been deceived, but he had no time. He had to get back to Ephesus as quickly as possible. He promised his faithful converts that he would come back quickly and stay longer, then he sailed for Ephesus, heartbroken, angry, and full of foreboding.

As he had feared, his enemies in Ephesus had used his absence to work up feeling against him. The feast of Artemis, the great goddess of Ephesus, was coming. During the feast, thousands of little silver models of the famous temple of Artemis were sold to pilgrims as souvenirs. The silversmiths of Ephesus made a good living out of selling these, and they were furious with the Christians for preaching that their gods and goddesses were fakes. They wanted to get rid of the Christians as quickly as possible. Feelings were running very high.

PAUL BOASTS OF HIS WEAKNESS

Paul was still preaching and arguing with his enemies. At the same time he wrote a letter to Corinth, a very angry and sorrowful letter. Much of this letter is lost, but possibly we still have some of it in the last four chapters of 2 Corinthians. These chapters obviously don't "belong" with the ones that go before it, and they are the kind of thing we would expect Paul to have written at that time. You can see from it that he was beside himself with worry about the Corinthians and the trouble that was brewing for the Church in Ephesus. Probably he was overworking as usual and didn't sleep enough. He wrote with savage irony against the people who defied his authority, who said he "bullied—but only by letter," who preached a "new" gospel, saying they were the true Jews, the true apostles and servants of Christ.

"These people are pretense apostles, cheating workmen disguised as apostles of Christ," he wrote.

"But let no one take me for a fool—or if you must, treat me as a fool and let me do a little boasting—like them. You are wise men, you can cheerfully put up with fools—even one who makes slaves of you, makes you feed him, orders you about, slaps you in the

58

Herbert G. May
A replica of an image of Artemis (Diana),
the fertility goddess of the Ephesians

face! It's a shame, isn't it, that we were weak with you, and didn't do this?

"I can boast as much as anyone. Are they servants of Christ? I must be mad to say this—but so am I and even more so, because I've worked harder, been oftener in prison, whipped, stoned, ship-wrecked, in constant danger."

He told them, though, that the only thing really worth boasting about was his weakness, because God could show his power in it. Even the wonderful visions he had had were not important: "For it is when I am weak that I am strong!"

Yet for all his anger Paul's love for them breaks through.

"I am quite willing to spend myself altogether, for your sakes. Because I love you more, must I be loved less?

"You say you want proof of Christ's power, shown in me? You say *he's* no weakling, like me? Yes, but first he was weak enough to be crucified, and he lives now by the power of God. So then, we are weak, as he was, but we shall live with him, through the power of God, for your sakes.

"We are only too glad to be weak, if only you are strong! We pray for you to be made perfect. That's why I am writing from far off, so that when I come I shouldn't need to be severe. The author-ity which the Lord gave me is for building up, not for breaking down."

It was Titus who took this letter to Corinth. This time Paul's sorrow and bitterness, and his love that would not give up in spite of all they had done, did overcome the opposition. The Corinthians realized how misled they had been. They were deeply sorry for what they had done, and they turned on the man who had led them against Paul and refused to have anything to do with him. They waited hopefully for Paul's next visit, for Paul had arranged to come to Corinth by land, meeting Titus at Troas on the way.

THE SILVERSMITHS' RIOT

But things had been moving fast in Ephesus. The silversmiths provoked a riot against the Church, the whole city was in an up-roar, and the believers persuaded Paul, for his own safety, to leave at once. So Paul set out for Troas, to meet Titus. But since Paul had left Ephesus sooner than he had meant to do, Titus was not there. Paul couldn't stand the delay. He was remembering the things he had said in his letter. Had he been too fierce? Would the Corinthians be provoked to worse rebellion? What would they do to Titus? Or did they think he no longer cared for them, that he had cast them off? Supposing they lost the faith altogether? Would it be his fault? He could not stand the suspense, although he could see that there was plenty of work to be done in spreading the good news in Troas. Later, he was to write to Corinth: "The door was wide open for my work in the Lord, but I was so uneasy in my mind at not meeting brother Titus there that I went on to Macedonia."

There was trouble in Macedonia, "quarrels outside, misgivings inside," as Paul said. But then Titus arrived with the good news from Corinth, and in his relief and joy Paul sent a letter to Corinth that must have more than made up for the angry one before. (This letter makes up most of what is in your Bible as 2 Corinthians.) Paul realized that he could not go straight to Corinth as he had meant to do; there was too much to be done in Macedonia. Besides, when he had first planned to go on to Corinth, he still thought he might have to threaten and punish the Corinthians and had written in the hope of avoiding this.

"I wrote as I did to make sure that when I came, I would not be made miserable by the very people who should have made me happy."

Paul seems so anxious to put everything right. Perhaps he was regretting the strong letter he had written. Even the man who had been the chief cause of the trouble must be forgiven: "The punishment imposed on him is enough—forgive him and encourage him now, or he might break down under so much misery." Paul knew what it was like to be despised and avoided, and he was generous enough to want to spare his old enemy. "I ask you to prove your love for him—anybody that you forgive, I forgive. As for *my* forgiving anything, if there *was* anything to forgive I have already forgiven it, for your sake, in the presence of Christ."

Paul could not go to Corinth just then—but the letter of reconciliation is so full of joy and confidence that it must have seemed almost as good as a visit. He keeps on saying how weak he is, and how glad he is to be weak, because it shows God's power.

"For it is not ourselves we are preaching, but Christ Jesus as the Lord, and ourselves as your servants for Jesus' sake.

"We are in difficulties on all sides, but never cornered, we see no answer to our problems, but never despair."
The middle part of this letter is almost a hymn of praise to God, for the power that comes to men through Christ and for the hope of glory and of longing for the completion of the work of Christ. Yet already, "for anyone who is in Christ, there is a new creation, the old one is gone, and already the new one is here. The day of salvation is *now!*"

Herbert G. May
A modern house with the Acrocorinth, or acropolis of Corinth, on the hilltop in the background. On the Acrocorinth was a famous temple of the goddess Aphrodite.

He kept coming back to his joy and relief, because his dear, foolish Corinthians were once more one in love and faith. "I have enormous confidence in you," he wrote—and only a few weeks before they had been insulting him! "I am so proud of you that in all our trouble here I am still overflowing with consolation and joy."

62

TO KNOW PAUL BETTER

To help yourself remember the journeys of Paul, look over your map. Check and make certain that all the places mentioned in this chapter are marked on the map. Mark in the route traveled by Paul from Ephesus to Corinth.

Does it seem that wherever Paul went he stirred up trouble? Why did the silversmiths of Ephesus riot? In what other cities that Paul visited had there been trouble?

9 Paul to the Romans

The longest, the most famous, and the most important of all Paul's letters is the one he wrote to the church at Rome. He wrote it during the winter of the year A.D. 57–58, after he had finally come back to Corinth.

After he had had to leave Ephesus he had been traveling about in Macedonia, visiting the Churches there and dealing with various kinds of trouble. There was the usual trouble from Jewish Christians, and also trouble from pagan converts who thought their baptism meant they could stop all personal effort at holiness and do whatever they liked. It took Paul all the rest of the summer to make his tour of the cities in Macedonia where there were Churches, and it was winter before he reached Corinth. He was glad to be back there, and the Church welcomed him warmly, but he knew he must not stay long. He was looking ahead, making plans. In Corinth he could easily get news from the west, and he heard how the Church in Rome was growing. He felt it was time he went to Rome. He had never been there, for the Church in Rome had been established for some time, and Paul did not usually visit a city unless he hoped to found a Church there, or else was visiting one he had founded. Why did he decide to go to Rome? Why did he write his most important letter to the Christians at Rome, people whom he had never met?

ROME, THE CENTER OF THE WORLD

Rome was the center of the Empire. It was the most important city in the world to the people of the Empire. Paul was a Jew, and he did not think of Rome as holy, as the pagans did, but he knew that if the good news was to reach all nations, as Christ had commanded, there must be a strong and fervent Church in Rome, and one that fully understood the message of Jesus.

This was important for two reasons. First, the Romans had arranged all their roads so that they led out from Rome to the various provinces. There were very few roads connecting the provinces with each other, and this was deliberate. It was meant to make it

View along the Appian Way, one of the many excellent roads that connected the Roman Empire in the time of Paul

difficult for different provinces to get together and rebel against Rome. So if one wanted messages or travelers to go to many countries, the best way was to send them out from Rome. (See map on page 84.)

The second reason was that Rome was not only the center of government but, like all capital cities, the center of fashions—fashions in clothes, of course, but also fashions in ideas, books, religions! If a new idea caught on in Rome, you could be sure that before long it would travel along those marvelous roads and in only a few months the provinces, too, would be wearing the new hairstyles, arguing about the new philosophy, telling the new joke, worshiping the new god, or dosing themselves with the new medicine! Paul knew all this. He was a Roman citizen; he knew how good the Roman law and the Roman roads were. He knew that the Roman law could be used to oppress, and the roads could carry evil ideas and silly fashions—but he also knew that the law would protect the messengers of the gospel, and the roads would take them to the very farthest edges of the Empire. But they must start out from Rome, for if the gospel was strong there it would be carried into the provinces with all the prestige of anything that came from Rome.

This was why Paul felt he must go to Rome. He meant to go back first of all to Jerusalem, to consult the other apostles about his plans. Then he would go to Rome, and after that to Spain.

But there were difficulties. Other people had brought the faith to Rome, and the Church there might not welcome Paul, who had a reputation for stirring up trouble! There were quite a few Christian leaders who disapproved of Paul and thought his teaching very odd, to say the least. If Paul wanted his teaching to spread from Rome it was important that the Roman Church should approve of him. So he decided to write to them beforehand and explain as clearly as he could the things in his teaching that people found puzzling or peculiar.

Paul took a great deal of trouble over his letter to the Romans. Although people have wondered how much he really wrote of some of his other letters, no one wonders about this one. All that is most "Pauline" comes out in this letter—the deep feeling, the new and unusual ways of thinking, the way he would pick up *any* kind of ideas that people were used to, and use them to explain his meaning. And there is his Jewish way of basing his arguments on passages or events in the Bible, as well as his own habit of jumping from one idea to another, leaving out the linking explanations, in a way that is often extremely bewildering to read. And most of all, even when this letter is most carefully thought out, his enthusiasm and his impatience, his faith and his love of Jesus Christ, keep breaking through, as if the things he was telling the Church were so wonderful that he was overcome with the joy and splendor of it all.

You may have wondered, in reading this book, how Paul managed to write to people in so many different countries. How did he know so many different languages? Or were his letters translated? In fact, he didn't need to know many languages, or get his letters translated, because nearly everyone in the Empire spoke Greek as well as his own language. It was not the elegant, classical Greek of the great Greek poets and writers, but a common sort of "business" Greek, called *koine* Greek. Just as the Roman roads and government joined many nations, so this *koine* Greek language was also a link between them. Just at this moment of history when it was needed to spread the gospel, it was very useful to have so widespread a common language.

H. Thomas Frank
Arch of Titus in Rome, center of the world in the time of Paul

WHAT MAKES PEOPLE HOLY?

Most of the letter to the Romans is taken up by trying to settle once and for all this question: What makes people holy? Is it obeying the Law, or is it faith in Christ? This may see like an old argument between the Christians who were Jews and those who weren't, but actually it is a very important question and bothers Christians just as much now as it did then.

Paul tried to explain this problem in his letter. There were educated and uneducated people in the Roman Church, Jews, Greeks, Romans, and "barbarians" (people from the provinces). To all of them, Paul said, he wanted to bring the good news, "the power of God saving all who have faith."

But if the good news brought light and life to those who believed, it must also show up much more strongly the wickedness of those who did not believe. If you live always in twilight, you get used to it, but if someone lights a lamp for you, the dark parts of the room look much darker. Yet even in twilight you ought to be able to see your way about and to walk properly. So even the pagans were able to see the things God had made, and recognize his power in them, if they tried.

"That is why there is no excuse for such people," wrote Paul. "They 'knew' God, yet they would not honor or thank him. They were so pleased with their own cleverness, it became a nonsense, and their silly minds grew darker and darker."

Since they could not see properly—*would* not see—naturally they could not understand how to live, and fell into every kind of sin and misery; this was a truth you could see all around you in a city like Rome. But were the Jews, who had been shown God's Law and knew clearly what was right, any better? They are as bad, if not worse, Paul says. They criticize the pagans, but they are condemned too, because they ought to know better.

"It isn't *listening* to the Law, its *keeping* it that will make people holy. And pagans who have never heard of the Law and yet do right are keeping the Law, the Law which is written in their hearts."

In that case, who is better off in God's sight, Jew or pagan? Neither, says Paul—Jews or Greeks, it's all the same—"*all* are under the power of sin." The fact remains that whether the Law is the written Law of Moses, or your conscience telling you what is right, it is not possible to do right. "No one can be justified in the sight of God by keeping the Law—all that the Law does is to tell you what is wrong."

Publishers Photo Service
The Forum on the Sacred Way, in Rome. From the Forum and the city of Rome ideas and laws went out to the provinces.

This is how Paul begins his letter—a very depressing beginning. Yet we all know it's true. It's one thing to know what you ought to do, quite another to *do* it. Then how can anyone be "justified"? "Justified" doesn't mean "seeming to be right"; it means belonging to God, sharing his life, being really and truly free, not afraid. It means, in fact, being what human beings are *meant* to be—but can't be, however hard they try. What's the use, then? Is it hopeless? No, says Paul. He began his letter in that depressing way on purpose. He wanted people to realize just how black the situation is, so that the hope he showed them would be all the more wonderful.

To learn more about the world in which Paul lived and taught, read about Rome as a city during Paul's life. Mark the main Roman roads on your map. If the roads go off the edge of the map, indicate the direction they go and to what city or country.

In Paul's time nearly everyone in the Roman Empire spoke koine *Greek, a sort of "business" Greek. This common language provided a link between the people of the Empire, just as the roads provided a link between the cities. Much later the British Empire also carried a common language to many parts of the world. How many countries can you name where English is spoken today, either as the main language or as a second language?*

10 Faith and Law

In the letter to the Roman Church, Paul set out the questions that are at the heart of Christian teaching.

He began by describing the wretched state of man when he turns away from God, and he sums up the situation and gives God's answer to it in one grand but extraordinary sentence: "Both Jew and pagan have sinned, and are without God's presence, but both are justified by a freely given grace, by being redeemed in Christ Jesus, who was appointed by God to sacrifice his life so as to win reconciliation through faith."

"Justified" is an odd word that means, as was explained at the end of the last chapter, being-with-God-in-the-right-way—not afraid, that is, or cut off by sin, but being in God's presence, in love, *sharing* his life which is also our own. It is how human beings are *meant* to be—but somehow can't be, by their own efforts alone. But they *can* be "reconciled," which means "put right," "brought together again," through Christ's cross, by *faith*.

Faith means trusting yourself to God, even though you can't see any reason to do so. Abraham, who obeyed God's command to leave his home and travel into a strange country, for no good reason anyone could think of, had faith. Was Abraham justified because he obeyed a law? No, says Paul, he was justified, he became God's friend, because he had faith, because he trusted God. The promise was made to Abraham because of his faith, not because of any law, for since Abraham lived before Moses to whom the Law was given, there *was* no Law then. That is why we say that Abraham is the father of *all* who believe. Our faith, too, will "justify" us if we believe in him who raised Jesus our Lord from the dead, Jesus who was put to death for our sins and raised to life to justify us, and to let us share in his risen life.

SIN, DEATH—AND LIFE

But how does this happen? Paul tried to explain this by talking of two kinds of men, who portray opposite ideas of what a human being is like: Adam and Christ. Sin came into the world through

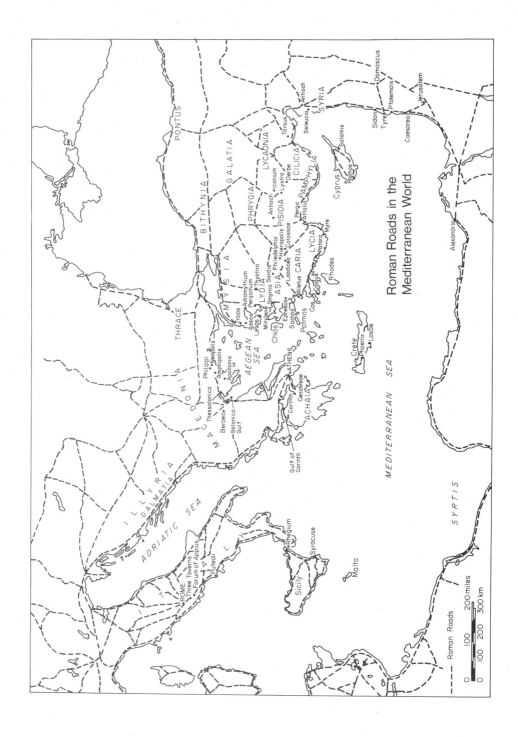

Roman Roads in the
Mediterranean World

Roman Roads

0   100   200 miles
0   100   200   300 km

one man, and sin means that creation is being *undone,* becoming nothing. Where there is sin, it is as if nothingness, *death,* ruled over everything. Sin isn't just a matter of breaking the Law. After all, the Law came with Moses, yet long before Moses there was sin, and it was "death that reigned over all."

"But if *death* ruled because of one man's fall, it is even more certain that one man, Jesus Christ, will make each one reign in *life,* if he accepts the entirely undeserved gift of sharing God's life.

"When the Law did come, it could only make more and more chances for people to sin—but however many sins there are, grace is even greater."

But then, some people might say, if grace is always greater than sin, shouldn't we go on sinning, to make sure of even more grace? "Of course not!" says Paul.

"We are dead to sin, so how can we go on living in it? When we were baptized it's as if we were buried with Christ, we shared his death. Then, just as Christ was raised from the dead by the Father's glory, we too may have a new kind of life.

"In that case, we are free from the Law. Does that mean that the Law is a kind of sin? Of course not—but I would not know what *was* sinful except through the Law. And once I knew, that made me *want* to sin, as if sin took the chance the Law gave it, to 'kill' me."

"I DO WHAT I DON'T WANT TO DO"

The Law itself is good, it is "spiritual," Paul says. What does he mean by spiritual? It is important to understand this, because he uses the word often. It doesn't mean that there is a something called "soul" or "spirit" inside you. Your spirit is really *yourself,* your most *real* self. But we don't always live in a *real* way because we are distracted by things we don't understand and are afraid of. We don't understand ourselves or our feelings; we get confused and angry and frightened. These are "unspiritual" feelings and behavior; they stop us being our true selves. Our real self, our spirit, is alive with the life that God gave us—his *own* life, his *own* Spirit, which we share through Christ.

So when Paul says the Law is "spiritual," he means that the good and sensible rules that we obey are a help to us in trying to become our real selves. These rules can't *make* us spiritual; they can only show us what's wrong.

Paul is speaking for every human being when he says: "I can't understand my own behavior. I don't do the things I really want to do, and I find myself doing things I hate! The fact is, I know of nothing good living in me—in my *un*spiritual self, that is, for though I *want* to do good, I do the sinful things I *don't* want to do! So it is not my true self doing it, but the sin that lives in me. In my heart I really love God's Law, but my feelings follow a different 'law,' that fights against the law that my mind tells me to obey. This is what makes me a prisoner!

"But the law of the spirit of life in Christ Jesus has set you free from the law of sin and death! God has done what the Law (because we are of the flesh, *unspiritual*) could not do. God dealt with this by sending his own Son as a real human being just like ourselves, whose flesh is sinful—and so he condemned sin in the flesh. [When Paul uses the word "flesh" he doesn't mean just "body" but ourselves as we are when we are *un*spiritual, that is, afraid and not understanding ourselves and so sinful.]

"So then, my brothers, we don't have to obey the flesh and live unspiritual lives. The spirit that has been given is not the spirit of slaves, making you fall back into fear again. It is the spirit of sons, it makes us cry out 'Father!'

"In that case, *nothing* can come between us and the love of Christ—no troubles or worries or persecution or lack of food or clothes, or danger.

"For I am certain that neither death nor life, nor angels nor princes, nothing that exists, now or in the future, not any power, or height or depth—nothing created at all—can ever come between us and the love of God which has been shown to us in Christ Jesus our Lord."

THE JEWS BELONG IN GOD'S PLAN

After this great, triumphant cry of faith, Paul's letter to the Romans calms down. In the next chapters (9 to 11) he tried to explain how the Jews did have a special place in God's plan, although the new life was meant for all. The Jews were the ones whom God chose and prepared for the coming of his Son. They are his special people. Although many refused to believe in the promised Savior when at last he came, still God would never cast them off. In the end, they must come back to him.

After this, Paul ended his letter quietly and affectionately, telling how he thought a man who has been brought into this new life should live.

Israel Office of Information
The Torah, symbol of an age-old spiritual heritage. Paul, teaching both Jew and pagan, was deeply aware of this heritage.

Toge Fujihira, Methodist Missions
"Love one another."

"Think of God's goodness, my brothers, and worship him in a spiritual way (not like the pagans) by giving yourselves to God, as a holy sacrifice, which is what he really wants of you. Don't copy the behavior of the world around you, but be changed by your new way of thinking.

"Love one another, as brothers should. Work hard for the Lord, be happy in your hope, do not give up if troubles come, and keep on praying. Bless people who are unkind to you—bless, not curse. Rejoice with those who rejoice, be sad with those who sorrow. Treat everyone with equal kindness; don't be condescending but really make friends with the poor. Never be smug. Try to live at peace with everyone.

"Obey the law of the country. If you behave well you need not be afraid of magistrates. The State is there to serve God, for your good. You should obey for conscience' sake, not just for fear of punishment. And so you should pay your taxes, too.

"Don't get into debt—except the debt of love that you owe one another! All the commandments are summed up in this one command—you must love your neighbor as yourself.

"For, you know 'the time' has come. [Paul means the new time, the day of the Lord, which has begun in Christ, when he rose from the dead.] You must wake up now! The night is almost over, the day is here—let us give up doing things that should only be done in the dark. Let us put on the armor of light."

We should be careful of each other's consciences—if one person feels uncomfortable about doing something we know is quite harmless, then it may harm *him* if he does or if he sees us do it.

We should not do things that could worry other people, even if they don't harm *us*.

"For the kingdom of God doesn't mean eating or drinking this or that, but goodness and peace and joy, through the Holy Spirit.

"Each of us should think of his neighbor and help him. Christ did not think of himself. It can only be to God's glory, then, for you to treat one another as Christ treated you.

"May the God of hope bring you such joy and peace in your faith that the power of the Holy Spirit may give you hope without limit."

TO KNOW PAUL BETTER

Think about Paul's references to Abraham. Why did the Jews refer to Abraham as their "father"? Look up the story of Abraham in the book of Genesis, and see how many other references to him you can find in other books of the Bible.

Who were the chief writers and philosophers whose work was popular in Rome at the time Paul was writing his letter to the Romans? What sort of ideas were they expressing? Did those ideas have any points in common with Paul's?

11 How Paul's Plans Were Upset

The person to whom Paul dictated his long letter to the Roman Church was a young man called Tertius. When he had finished saying all that he wanted to say, he still wondered, "Will they think it strange that I should be writing all this to them? Will they be offended because I seem to be telling them the good news as if they didn't already know it? Or will they wonder why I haven't visited them before, and feel slighted?" So he added on an extra, more personal bit, to tell them his reasons once more, and his plans for the future.

Herbert G. May
Excavated theater at Miletus. Paul called the elders of Ephesus to Miletus and spoke to them.

"I have not written because I have any doubts about you—I am sure you are full of goodness and able to teach one another. The reason I have written—perhaps rather forcefully—is to remind you about certain things, since God has given me a special work as a servant of Jesus Christ, the priestly work of bringing the good news of God to the pagans.

"I have some reason to be proud of what, in Christ, I have done for God. But it is only what Christ himself has done to win the faith of the pagans, using what I have said and done. I have preached the good news all the way from Jerusalem to Illyricum, as well as I possibly could. But I have made it a rule not to preach where the name of Christ has already been heard; I didn't want to build on other men's foundations. That is what kept me from visiting you before, although I have wanted to for years. Now, however, I have finished my work here [he meant he had founded the Church, and would leave others to build on his foundations] and I hope to see you on my way to Spain. Only first I have to take some money to the saints [this was the usual word for Christians, God's holy people] at Jerusalem, a present to the poor there from Macedonia and Achaia. But I beg you, brothers, to help me by your prayers—pray that I may escape the unbelievers in Judea. May the God of peace be with you all."

THE LETTER COPIED FOR OTHER CHURCHES

We can see from this that Paul was expecting trouble in Judea, and was afraid of it. He knew he had deadly enemies there, and felt he might never again see some of the Churches he had founded. When he thought of this he wondered if, when he was gone, they would forget his teaching. The odd letters he had sent them from time to time were not enough, since they had often been written in a hurry. The only one that he had taken time over and thought out carefully was the one he had just finished, for the Roman Church. The teaching in it did not just apply to the Romans, but could be for any of the believers. So Paul decided to send copies of this letter to other Churches as well. He asked Tertius to copy it and send it to them, and with each copy to add a little extra note, putting in personal greetings and messages for the particular Church to which the copy was going.

As it is in your Bible, the last passages of the Letter to the Romans (chapter 16) seems to be one of these "covering letters." It sends greetings to two people you know about already—Priscilla and Aquila who had stayed behind when Paul had left

Ephesus at the time of the silversmiths' riots. The letter to the Romans was written only six months after this, and it seems likely that they were still in Ephesus. Paul says, in this last passage, that they "risked death to save my life," and presumably he is referring to the riots.

We can assume, then, that the copy of the letter to the Romans that is in our Bibles is the one sent to Ephesus, and that it was taken there by a woman, Phoebe, who lived at the port of Cenchreae, and was a deaconess of the Church there. (We are told all this at the beginning of chapter 16.) Deaconesses were women specially chosen and blessed to serve the Church in works of charity and also in worship, just as the deacons (men) also did. Paul wrote of Phoebe: "Give her a welcome worthy of saints and help her with anything she needs. She has looked after a great many people, myself included."

Then follows a long list of people to whom Paul sends greetings, with one Jewish name (Mary) among all the Greek ones. One of the people mentioned is Rufus, who may have been the son of Simon of Cyrene, the countryman who helped Jesus to carry his cross. Paul says of Rufus, "His mother has been a mother to me too."

"Timothy, who is working with me, sends his greetings, so do Jason and Sosipater, who are of my own people." Then comes a little note from the actual writer of the letter: "I, Tertius, who wrote out this letter, greet you in the Lord."

All these messages and greetings make us feel how much of a *family* these first Christians were. They had their quarrels and troubles, certainly, but they also shared this warm friendliness and hospitality. Any believer was sure of a welcome in any Christian household, at any time. Paul didn't just *talk* about love, he made people feel the love of Christ so strongly in him that they wanted to live by it themselves. They opened their minds to his message, and so the love by which Paul lived—the love of Christ—became theirs also. It grew and spread, and everyone who met it felt its warmth—the fire of the Spirit. People said to each other, "See how these Christians love one another!" And that is how people ought to recognize Christians, as Christ had told them: "By this men will know that you are my disciples—that you love one another."

Israel Office of Information
A scale model of Old Jerusalem

But Paul had to carry that message further. As he said in a little prayer at the end of this letter: "Glory to him who is able to give you strength to live by the good news I preach, and in which I proclaim Jesus Christ, uncovering a mystery that has been secret for endless ages, but is now so clear that it must be told to all nations, to bring them to faith as God has commanded!" Paul had to move on to other nations, though his plan did not turn out exactly as he had expected.

THE JOURNEY TO JERUSALEM

He had meant to go straight to Syria, on his way to Jerusalem, but a sudden change of plan became essential. One of the brothers brought news of a plot to kill Paul: some of the Jews in Judea, who hated Paul as the greatest enemy of their religion, were planning to kill him on board ship during the voyage. If they did it quietly, perhaps during rough weather (it was spring, a stormy time of year), they could drop his body overboard with no questions asked.

So Paul went overland instead, and perhaps he was glad of the chance to visit old friends en route, even so briefly. He knew he might never see them again. Wherever he went crowds of believers flocked to see him and listen to him, and were prepared to sit up all night. At Troas, for instance, he preached until morning, and celebrated the Lord's Supper with them. At dawn he set off again. He did not go to Ephesus, for he was in a hurry, hoping to be in Jerusalem at Pentecost, but some Christians came out from Ephesus to see him at Miletus. They wept and embraced him, and prayed for his safety. Then they saw him off to his ship. (Follow this journey on the map on page 36.)

Luke was with Paul on this journey—when he wrote the Acts of the Apostles he recorded every port at which they called. (Luke was interested in ships and navigation, and he always remembered this kind of detail.) Luke later told the story of Paul's strange adventures after he reached Jerusalem, for all Paul's plans went wrong. He did come to Rome, as he had planned, but he came as a prisoner.

PRISONER OF THE ROMANS

Paul's Jewish enemies would stop at nothing to get rid of him. To them, he was the worst kind of traitor, for he had been a Pharisee—a member of a Jewish sect who followed the Law with extreme strictness—and was now preaching that the Law of Moses was not essential for holiness! In Jerusalem, when he went to the Temple to pray, they provoked a riot against him; when Roman troops rescued him, they brought wild accusations against him, saying he was a rebel against Rome. Paul was a Roman citizen, and the Roman troops were bound to protect him until he could be properly tried. But Paul's enemies vowed to ambush and kill him while he was being taken to face his accusers at the Council of the Sanhedrin. Luckily a nephew of Paul's found this out and told the Roman officer, who decided to send Paul under armed guard to Felix, the Roman governor, at Caesarea.

But Felix delayed action and would not bring the case to trial. He didn't want to offend the Jews, but on the other hand he was impressed by Paul, and also he hoped Paul might offer him money!

So in the end nothing happened. Paul remained a prisoner in Caesarea for two years, until another governor, called Festus, was appointed. He reopened the case. But Paul knew he would not be likely to get a fair hearing, for the Jews would bring lying witnesses against him, and Festus' real concern was in keeping the country quiet. So Paul did what every Roman citizen had the right to do if he felt he was being unjustly accused: he appealed to Rome.

"I appeal to Caesar," he told Festus.

"You have appealed to Caesar, to Caesar you shall go," Festus replied.

TO KNOW PAUL BETTER

At the beginning and end of most of Paul's letters are greetings and messages to and from various people. Some names appear over and over again. List six or seven of these and think about how Paul trusted these people and how much they helped him in his work. Who were these people, where were they from, and what work did they do?

Find these names also in the Acts of the Apostles, and note what actions of theirs are recorded there.

Look up the places mentioned in this chapter and mark them on your map. Mark also the provinces of the Roman Empire.

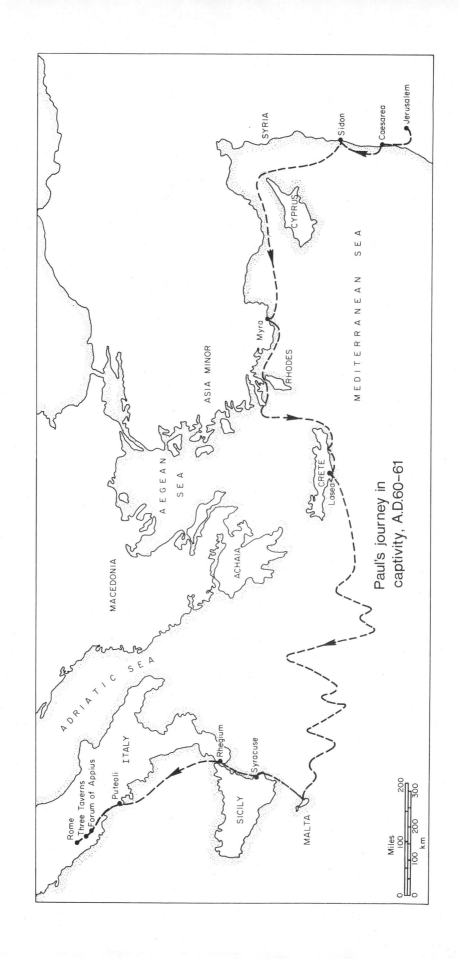

Paul's journey in
captivity, A.D.60–61

12 Paul at the Heart of the Empire_____

Even the journey to Rome did not go according to plan. In the autumn of A.D. 60, Paul was sent off under guard, but the ship was wrecked on the island of Malta, and although no one was killed, the ship itself was smashed to bits. It was now winter, and because there were no more ships goings on to Italy in such rough weather, Paul stayed in Malta until the spring. When the good weather came, he and his guard sailed to Puteoli in Italy, and then traveled to Rome. Paul had reached the heart of the Empire at last, but in chains.

Paul had appealed to Caesar, which meant that his case was to be tried by the emperor himself, who at that time was Nero. (Nero is said to have played his lyre while Rome burned, but that is only a legend. He was, all the same, a slightly mad and very unpleasant man.) There were a great many cases waiting to be heard by the emperor, and Nero was in no hurry. Paul remained a prisoner, waiting for his trial, for about two years. He was not held in a prison, but was allowed to live in a house of his own, which was carefully guarded. He was allowed to have visitors and send letters. In fact, he could do as he liked, provided he did not leave the house.

This suited Paul very well. He was able to talk to the Christians of Rome, explain his teaching, encourage believers, and preach the gospel to others who had never heard it, but had heard of Paul. The Jews in Rome came to listen to him with open minds, untroubled by the disputes that had divided the Judeans. Some of them were convinced by what he said, but others would not believe him. "The foreigners will listen to me!" he told these unbelievers, and he was right. They did.

Helping Paul with his work in Rome were several people you have heard of already—Luke, Timothy, Mark. Paul mentioned them in the letters he wrote now, and sent greetings from them.

Herbert G. May
Tradition places here the site of Paul's imprisonment in Rome

There are three letters in your Bible that belong to this part of Paul's life when he was under house arrest in Rome. They were sent to the Colossians, the Ephesians, and to Philemon. The first two are so different from the earlier letters that many people have wondered whether it was really Paul who wrote them. If he didn't, then there must have been someone else writing who was as great and brilliant a thinker as Paul. If that was so, it seems odd that nobody mentioned him or remembered him! Scholars are still trying to settle the matter, and probably we shall never know for certain, but it is *possible* that it all happened as I shall explain here. You can decide for yourself whether this account fits what you know about Paul and his writing.

The Church at Colossae had not been founded by Paul, but by a disciple of his called Epaphras or Epaphroditus. (He was the one who was ill at Ephesus, and was sent back to Philippi when he got better.) Epaphras came to Rome to see Paul, and to ask for his help in settling some arguments that were disturbing the Colossian Church. These particular questions were not ones Paul had had to deal with before, and this is one reason why the letter he now wrote is very different from his earlier ones. Also, since he was a prisoner and had to stay put whether he liked it or not, he was not writing in a hurry, but in a more leisurely way. Besides, he was getting older, and no longer felt that everything could be done at once! Paul the impatient was learning to wait, and that was probably the hardest lesson he ever had to learn.

The matter worrying the Church at Colossae was something that was going to trouble the Churches, one way or another, for centuries to come.

Paul was told that the Christians in Colossae were being influenced by a strange "mystery" religion, many forms of which were current in Asia at that time. These religions thought of God as so completely unattainable that they worshiped "angels" instead— though they did not call them angels but "Powers," "Dominations," "Sovereignties," and so on. Some of them also worshiped Christ, but only as one of these powers, sent by God, as they were, to bring "knowledge" to men, to set them free from the kingdom of darkness and bring them into the kingdom of light.

The idea behind all this teaching was that a person could be saved and made holy only by knowing certain secret and mysterious teachings. Faith and love would not free a person from sin: only this secret knowledge would.

People who followed these teachings often had very strict rules about food, and about keeping certain fast days and holy days. In fact, they treated their bodies severely, and led very rigorous lives, because they thought that the body was evil, keeping the "good" soul shut up in it until it was set free by the mysterious "knowledge."

Now some parts of this kind of teaching did seem rather like some of Paul's own teaching; for example, he often said that Christians should not be self-indulgent, but should care for *spiritual* things above all. But Paul always taught that the body was *good,* and that it should be treated with respect and not ill used or wasted, because it was good. A man is *one whole,* body and soul, and it is this whole that will be transformed in Christ, not just the soul. So Paul was very distressed to hear of this twisting of the true teaching, and he wrote to the Colossians at once to try to put things right.

In this letter Paul used the kind of words and ideas that the false teachings used. He knew that people would understand what he was saying more easily if he used the terms they were used to. He didn't mind if people believed that God worked through angels and Powers and so on, provided they realized that Christ was not just one of many angels, but was quite different. He was God's own Son, and man's only way to God and salvation came through faith in him, not through any kind of secret knowledge, let alone through ill-treating one's body.

"God has taken us out of the power of darkness, and created a place for us in the kingdom of the Son he loves—and in *him* we gain our freedom and the forgiveness of our sins.

"He is the image of the God we cannot see,
the first-born of all creation,
for in him were created all *things in heaven and earth,*
everything visible and *everything invisible—*
Thrones, Dominations, Sovereignties, Powers—

Herbert G. May
En route from Athens to Corinth, the Great Hall of Mysteries
at Eleusis, sanctuary of the outstanding pagan mystery cult

all *things were created through him and in him.*
Before anything was created, he was,
and he holds all things together in one.
Now the Church *is his body—*
he is its head.

"No one else but Jesus Christ can bring men to God, now he
has reconciled *you,* by his death, and it happened in his mortal
body. Now you are holy, as long as you stand firm in the *faith,*
not letting yourselves drift away from the hope promised by the
good news, which is preached to all creation—not just to special
'knowing' people.

"I'm glad to suffer for you, as I do suffer now in my own body
(because this carries on the work that Christ did by *his* suffering),
for the sake of his body, the Church.

"You must live your whole life by the Christ you have received
—Jesus, the Lord. You must be rooted in him and built on him.
Make sure no one traps you and takes away freedom by empty
'clever' philosophy, which belongs to this world, not to Christ. In

Publishers Photo Service

A restored private home of Pompeii. Paul may have been under house arrest in Rome in a
building like this.

his body the fullness of God really lives. You have been buried with him by baptism, and so raised up with him, by believing in the power of God who raised him from the dead!

"He has overruled the Law, he has canceled out our debt, by nailing it to the cross. From now onward, never let anyone decide what you are to eat or drink, or observe special days. These are only signs, the real thing is Christ. If you have really died with Christ, why do you still obey little rules—'don't touch this, or eat that!' All these have to do with things that soon perish, and anyway, they are merely human rules and regulations. But you really must get rid of behavior that ties you to this earthly life—things like impurity and greed. You have stripped off your old behavior with your old self, and you have put on a new self, which will go on toward the *true* 'knowledge.' You are God's chosen people, his saints. He loves you, and so you should be 'clothed' in kindness and humility and gentleness—and over all these 'clothes,' put on love! And so may the peace of Christ reign in your hearts."

This letter was taken to Colossae by a believer called Tychicus, who would also give the Church there the latest news about Paul and the rest of the Church at Rome. But the letter was also to be handed round to other Churches in that part of the world, because Paul knew they too were troubled by the same kind of false teaching.

A LETTER TO PHILEMON, THE SLAVE OWNER

With Tychicus went another man, a slave called Onesimus, and Paul sent a special letter about him (written by Paul himself) to his master, Philemon. This is the only letter we have that Paul wrote to a single person—the others were all meant to be read out to the Church and passed around. This letter is affectionate and easy; it shows how much real trust and love there was among the Christians. Onesimus had run away from his master, turned up in Rome, and been converted by Paul.

"I am appealing for this 'child' of mine, whose 'father' I became while I was wearing these chains. I am sending him back, and it seems as if I'm sending part of myself! I would have liked to have kept him here, to help me, but I don't want to do anything without your consent. You have had to do without him for a time, but only so that you could have him back forever, not as a slave, but as a dear brother—so if you care about all that we share, welcome him as if he were me. . . . I am sure you will do this, and more!"

TO KNOW PAUL BETTER

To learn more about the world Paul lived in, study the Roman emperors. Paul lived from about A.D. 10 to about A.D. 67. Make a list of the Roman emperors during those years, with the dates of their rule.

Find pictures and descriptions of a Roman house.

Mark on your map the route of Paul's journey from Caesarea to Rome.

Giorgetta Bell Signs of the Zodiac: a superstition many people still accept

13 A Letter to the Gentiles

Evidently Paul was hoping to be set free quite soon. At the end of his letter to Philemon he put a sort of P.S.: "One other thing—will you get a place ready for me to stay in? I'm hoping to come back to you, through your prayers."

Under Roman law, a citizen could be held in custody for two years awaiting trial. If by that time he had not been tried, he must be set free. It is assumed that this happened in Paul's case, and scholars think that after two years, during which no evidence was brought, he was freed in A.D. 63. He may then have traveled to Spain, or more probably back to Macedonia and Asia. He must have been imprisoned again, later, when Nero was persecuting the Christians fiercely, and he was probably executed about A.D. 67, but without exact evidence we can't be sure of the events of these years.

In any case, it is reasonable to suppose that Paul would have been anxious to make his teaching as clear as possible while he was still able to do so, and the theme of his letter to the Colossians did not leave him when that letter was finished.

While he was writing to Colossae, he probably discussed his letter with his friends in Rome, some of whom were learned and scholarly people. It seems likely, in fact, that he got someone who knew more about the "mystery" religions than he did to help him compose the letter. A pagan convert, perhaps one who had himself belonged to one of the mystery religions, would feel at home with such ideas. This may be why the letter to Colossae sounds so different from earlier ones, although its main ideas are very Pauline. The time he spent discussing this problem and writing the letter must have made Paul realize what a huge problem it was. Also, it made him think out his own teaching in a new way. Once before, when he had been dealing with the issues that bothered the Churches in Galatia (about Law and holiness) he had developed new ideas, and had then thought them out and expressed them more fully and clearly afterward, in his letter to the Romans. Now, though he had finished the letter to Colossae, he could not forget

Herman H. Kreider
The Taurus Mountains of Turkey, through which Paul passed
on his second and third missionary journeys. Paul's travels
took him many miles over land and sea.

the matter, and perhaps he thought it would be a good idea to set down a more careful explanation of his ideas.

WHO WROTE THE LETTER TO THE EPHESIANS?

The letter called "Ephesians" is this extra, more careful explanation. But the odd thing is that this letter does not really seem like Paul's work. It has his kind of teaching in it, certainly, but it is heavy and slow and complicated. Parts of it are taken straight out of the letter to Colossae—and Paul never repeated himself, his mind was always moving ahead. These borrowed extracts are put in rather awkwardly, as if the writer were not quite sure what they meant. It is all very solemn, never excitable. It never seems to take off as Paul did when he was thrilled by the wonders of the work of salvation. Yet the letter to the Ephesians contains ideas that seem to grow naturally out of what Paul had written before.

Did Paul write this letter? Of course, he never actually "wrote" any of his letters—except the little personal note to Philemon. He dictated them, often in a hurry, as we saw earlier. Perhaps this time he wasn't able to settle down and work out the letter in peace, as he did the one to the Romans. Perhaps he knew he had to leave Rome or might soon be executed, and he had a lot of business to get through—people to see, arrangements to make. Yet he was anxious that the letter should be written, for he knew it was important. So perhaps he explained his ideas to his "secretary"—who may have been the person who helped him with the letter to Colossae. He may have said, "Look, I haven't time to work it all out with you, but these are the main things I want to say, and if you can't remember look up that letter to Colossae. Do your best, this is important."

We can't be sure, but it could have happened like that. However it happened, the letter was written and sent to various Churches, about the same time as the letter to Colossae, and taken by the same person, Tychicus, though possibly it happened on another trip.

It begins, as usual, "From Paul, appointed by God to be an apostle of Jesus Christ, to the saints who are faithful to Christ Jesus —grace and peace to you."

In your Bible you may find the words, "the saints who are at

Ephesus." This is because the copy of the letter from which most copies were made was the one sent to Ephesus. That is why it is called "the letter to the Ephesians," though it was really meant for all the Gentile Churches, as they were the ones who might be influenced by the false teaching. There was probably a blank after "saints," where could be added the name of the Church to which the copy was going.

Many of the ideas in this letter are the same as those in the letter to the Colossians, which was explained in the last chapter. And it sums up, in many ways, earlier teaching as well. It constantly stresses: "It is by God's freely given love that you are saved, not by anything you have done. We are God's work, created in Jesus Christ to live the good life as we were meant to live it, from the beginning."

In Christ, Jews and pagans are drawn together, and the pagans share the promise made to Israel.

"For he is the peace between us, and has made two into one. He has made one single new man in himself out of the two of them, and by bringing peace through his cross he united them in a single body, and reconciled them with God.

"So you are no longer foreigners, you are part of God's family. You are part of a building that has the apostles and prophets for its 'foundations,' and Christ himself as its chief cornerstone. And you too are being built into a house where God lives, in the Spirit."

One part of this letter has kept for us another short passage from one of the hymns that Christians used to sing at that time. The letter says that Christians should be "children of light," the light of Christ which makes people really good and true, not mere pretenses of light like the secret "knowledge" which is really a darkness.

"Things that are done in secret must be things people are ashamed of. But anything exposed by the light will be lit up, and what is lit up becomes light—that is why we say:

Awake, O Sleeper, arise from the dead,
and Christ will shine on you!"

This particular hymn may have been used at baptism, which is an "awakening" from death to a new life, in Christ.

Herbert G. May
The harbor at Neapolis (modern Kavala, Greece) which served
as the port of Philippi, where Paul landed on his first trip to Europe

LOVE ONE ANOTHER, AS CHRIST LOVES

The letter ends, as the letter to Colossae does, with some advice about how Christians should live—married people, children, masters and slaves—all should love each other. But in this letter Paul (and surely this is *his* idea) takes up the idea about Christ making Jews and pagans *one* in his own body, the Church, and uses it in a different way. He uses it to explain why marriage is holy. This was important, because the mystery religions taught that since the body was evil, marriage was evil too.

"Give way to one another in obedience to Christ. Wives should think of their husbands as they think of the Lord, since Christ is the 'head' of his wife. . . . Husbands should love their wives just as Christ loved the Church and gave himself up for her, to make her holy. (And since 'holiness' means having God's life, the Church has Christ's life.) In the same way, husbands must love their wives as their own bodies; for a man, to love his wife is really to love *himself* . . . and that is the way Christ treats the Church, because it is his body, and we are its living parts. For this reason a man must leave his father and mother and be joined to his wife, and the two will become one single being [this is a quotation from the book of Genesis, in the Old Testament]. This mystery has many meanings, but here I am saying that it applies to Christ and the Church."

The letter ends with a passage in which the writer compares the Christian to a soldier, arming himself against the powers of evil— the "spiritual army of evil in the heavens" that the false teaching told people to worship. Perhaps Paul didn't write this—it is rather too elaborate for his kind of writing—but it is a stirring passage, and one that Christians have liked to dwell upon. Some of the phrases (those in quotation marks) come from the book of the prophet Isaiah:

"Stand firm, 'with truth buckled round your waist,' and 'honest thinking for your breast-plate,' wearing for shoes 'the eagerness to spread the gospel of peace,' and always carrying the shield of faith, so that you can use it to put out the burning arrows of evil. And then you must take 'salvation from God as your helmet' and the word of God brought to you by the Spirit must be your sword."

To get an overall view of Paul's letters and his work, make a list of all the letters. List where Paul was when he wrote each one. Give the dates at which they probably were written.

From reading about Paul and from what he says in his letters, what are the most important ideas that he taught? What sort of person was he?

14 The Church Founded on the Apostles____

Nobody knows for certain when Paul died, or how. Did he go traveling again? Perhaps. It may have been during these travels that he wrote to Timothy and to Titus to tell them how a leader and teacher of Christians should live. Certainly he must have written to them both from time to time, for they were both his devoted friends and disciples; they were the ones he trusted most completely to carry out the work in the way he had begun it. They were often away from him, sometimes for quite a long time. So it is likely that he wrote to them often.

TIMOTHY AND TITUS, PAUL'S FRIENDS

Are the three letters we have in our Bible—two to Timothy and one to Titus—actually the letters Paul sent? Many people think not. They don't sound very much like Paul. They are careful and cautious and always insisting on "sound teaching," whereas Paul used to talk of the "good news." Could Paul have changed so much in a couple of years? Perhaps he did—perhaps he was afraid that his work would be undone after his death, that new teachers would pull down what he had built up, and so he kept insisting on sound teaching and "tradition" and obedience. But Paul was a man of great faith. Could he really fear that the power of the Spirit that had driven him from one city to another, through every kind of danger, never giving up, would fail in the Church when he was dead? Surely not! And yet other passages in these letters do sound exactly like Paul, and, as we have seen, surely he did write to Timothy and Titus.

Let me suggest a likely solution to this puzzle. (It's not certain—you must decide for yourself whether you think it a likely one.)

Since the letters to Timothy and Titus were personal letters they would not be copied and handed round and carefully kept, like the letters to whole Churches. So it isn't surprising if they were torn and partly lost, and only bits of them survived. And before long it would be hard to say when these bits were written or exactly why. But they were Paul's letters, and therefore precious—even

J. Lane Miller
A Christian church on Rhodes, in the town of Lindos, not far
from where Paul landed en route to Jerusalem

more precious after he was dead and could write no more. And soon Timothy and Titus were dead also, and could not explain how the fragments of letters fitted in with each other.

AFTER THE DEATH OF THE APOSTLES

Meanwhile, the Church was changing. The apostles were dying —many of them martyred. Yet the end of all things had not come, as so many had expected. Clearly the old, sinful world was going to go on for some time yet. In that case, the Church must go on too, and must go on trying to bring the news of salvation to the world, even though the apostles were dead. Besides, the Church was growing—despite persecution, it kept growing. For both these reasons it was necessary to *organize* the local Churches more carefully. If the end of the world was coming any minute, organization could be quite simple, and the apostles (especially Paul) were there to settle difficulties as they arose. But if the Church had a long task ahead—and no apostles to help—something must be done to see that Christians lived according to their faith, and that this faith continued to be truly the faith preached by the apostles.

So each Church appointed an *episkopos*—a bishop—to rule it, with elders and deacons to help him. His chief work was to see to it that the *tradition*—the faith *handed on* by the apostles—was kept whole and clear and not mixed up with peculiar new teachings, such as the mystery religions.

When the leaders of the Church were trying to see that this was done, they found the remnants of Paul's letters to Timothy and Titus a great help, because Timothy and Titus had been leaders and teachers of the Churches, working with Paul, and his advice to them was still good advice. Besides, if it was *Paul's* advice everyone was bound to take notice, because Paul was not only one of the greatest of all the apostles, he was also the *only* apostle who had spent his whole preaching life working in the Greek and Roman world. And it was in *this* world, not in the Jewish world of Palestine, that the Church had to live.

This was especially important because in A.D. 70, soon after Paul's death, after much bitter fighting and a horrible siege, Jerusalem was entirely destroyed. The Jews were no longer a nation, only scattered refugees. Now there was no longer a "Church at Jerusalem," that could be referred to as the mother Church. From now on, the Church of Christ was an *European* Church, a *Roman* Church in fact, because to those who belonged to it the Empire seemed to be the whole world.

So perhaps it came about that the new leaders of the Church, the successors of the apostles, asked someone to put together what was left of Paul's letters to two of the "bishops" or leaders of his time, Timothy and Titus, and arrange them in a way that would be most helpful to people at that later time (probably between A.D. 70 and A.D. 90). He would fill in the gaps, and make sense of them, by writing in the kind of general instructions and warnings and greetings that he thought Paul would have written. After all, this was what Paul's "secretaries" had often done. But this time the Church the writer was seeing was a different kind of Church from the one Paul had worked in. He couldn't see with *Paul's* eyes, but wrote as he himself saw, for the Church *he* knew, a Church without the apostles, but anxious to keep their teaching and hand it on faithfully.

These three letters (the two to Timothy and the one to Titus) are called "Pastoral" letters, because they are about the shepherding of Christ's flock ("pastor" means shepherd). They are full of warning against false teachers: "During the last times there will be some who will desert the faith and choose to listen to deceitful spirits and doctrines that come from devils." These warnings are against the mystery teachings, which were now even more of a worry than they had been when Paul first attacked them.

But, for the most part, these letters contain good advice about how to treat people and help them to live as Christians. "Do not speak harshly to a man older than yourself, but advise him as if he were your father; treat younger men as brothers, and older women as you would your mother." There are rules for widows (who sometimes became a sort of nun) and for deacons and deaconesses.

The bishop—who in Paul's time did not rule, but was an "elder" who *presided* at, or *led* the assembly—must have a good character. He must not have been married more than once; he must be a moderate man, sensible and polite, hospitable and a good teacher.

Three Lions
A Greek priest from Cana near
Galilee. Paul and the Apostles
traveled near and far and helped
found churches everywhere they
went, in Palestine and
all over the Roman Empire.

These letters show that the writer is anxious to keep the Church unchanging and steady, and feels this is best done by keeping to the usual customs and laws, even though these are not specially Christian ones, but just the ordinary custom and laws of the land.

He keeps coming back to the need to stick to "sound teaching."

"Keep as your pattern the sound teaching you have heard from me, in the faith and love that are in Christ Jesus. You have been trusted to look after something precious—guard it with the help of the Holy Spirit who lives in us. . . . *Hand it on* to reliable people so that they in turn will be able to teach others."

In the second letter to Timothy is one sentence that seems to sum up both Paul's own preaching and the need to hand it on to later Christians. In this sentence there is a little bit from an early Christian "creed"—a declaration of faith, perhaps made at baptism by a new Christian: "Remember the good news that I carry —Jesus Christ, risen from the dead, sprung from the race of David."

Paul's whole life was given to God, in order to spread the good news that a new life had come into the world through Christ, who rose from the dead, uniting Jews (the race of David) and pagans in a new man. *"Remember,"* says Paul, "the good news I *carry."* He "carried" it and handed on what he carried, and this tradition has continued ever since: the tradition that we are called to share the life of God himself, through faith in Jesus Christ, who died for us and rose to a new life, which is ours, in him.

TO KNOW PAUL BETTER

As you think back on this book about Paul and his letters, think about the Churches he established. Do the letters show that Paul felt the Church should be kept unchanged by keeping to the usual customs and laws? Think about the structure of today's Church— the way in which it is organized, the ways in which its programs and ministries are handled. Should it be changed?

Name all those places where Paul established Churches and indicate the places on your map, if you have not already done so.

Read more about Paul's life and his world. Other books are listed on page 107.)

OTHER HELPFUL BOOKS

Bainton, Roland. *The Church of Our Fathers.* New York: Charles Scribner's Sons, 1950.

Bowie, Walter Russell. *The Bible Story for Boys and Girls.* Nashville: Abingdon Press, 1951.

Buckmaster, Henrietta. *Paul: A Man Who Changed the World.* New York: McGraw-Hill, 1965.

Cary, M., and others. *The Oxford Classical Dictionary.* Oxford: Clarendon Press, 1949.

Fosdick, Harry Emerson. *The Life of Saint Paul,* ill. by Leonard Fisher. New York: Random House, 1962.

Harvey, P. *The Oxford Companion to Classical Literature.* Oxford: Clarendon Press, 1967.

Kraeling, Emil G. *I Have Kept the Faith.* Chicago: Rand McNally, 1965.

Lillie, Amy Morris. *Run the Good Race,* ill. by Steele Savage. Nashville: Abingdon Press, 1965.

McKenzie, J. L. *Dictionary of the Bible.* London: Geoffrey Chapman, 1965.

Pittenger, W. Norman. *The Life of Saint Paul.* New York: Franklin Watts, 1968.

Terrien, Samuel. *The Golden Bible Atlas,* ill. by William Bolin. New York: Golden Press, 1957.

Wright, G. Ernest, and Floyd V. Filson, editors. *The Westminster Historical Atlas to the Bible.* Philadelphia: Westminster Press, 1956.

Young Readers Dictionary of the Bible. Nashville: Abingdon, 1969.

index

Abraham, 35, 71
Achaicus, 44
Antioch, 30, 31
Aphrodite, 15, 47, 62
Apollos, 39, 44, 45-46
apostles, 30, 32, 34, 37, 66, 101,
    103, 104
Aquila and Priscilla, 15, 39, 79
Artemis, 30, 57, 58, 59
Athens, 14, 16, 46

Beroea, 14, 19
Bible, 9, 11
bishop, bishops, 103, 104

Chloe, 44
circumcise, circumcision, 30, 32, 34,
    53
Claudius, Emperor, 15
Colossae, 87, 91, 94, 96
Colossians, Letter to, 87, 88, 89, 91
Corinth, 13-15, 17, 18, 20, 28, 38,
    39, 41, 43, 44, 45, 47, 49, 57,
    62, 63, 64
Corinthians, First Letter to, 41, 44-
    50
    Second Letter to, 57, 58, 60, 61, 62
    Lost Letter to, 41, 58
Crispus, 17

"day of the Lord," 23, 24
Diana, *see* Artemis
dictation of letters, 9, 11, 19-20, 27,
    38, 96-97

end of world, 20, 22-23, 103
Epaphroditus, 54, 87
Ephesians, Letter to, 87, 96-99
Ephesus, 30, 32, 38, 39, 42, 43, 49,
    52, 57, 60, 63, 64, 78, 80, 82,
    87
Erastus, 39, 41

Felix, 82
Festus, 82, 83
Fortunatus, 44

Galatia, 31, 32
Galatians, Letter to, 32, 34-36
Gallio, 26
Greek language, 67

hymns, 55, 62, 97-98

Jerusalem, 30, 31, 32, 33, 34, 37, 66,
    81, 82, 102
    destruction of, 103
    meetings of apostles, 30, 66
    mother Church, 104
Judaea, 79
justification, 69, 71

Law, Jewish, 30, 32, 34, 53, 68-69,
    73, 82
letter writing, 9-11, 19-20
Letters of Paul, *see* under name of
    each letter; *e.g., Thessalonians,
    Letter to*
Lord's Supper, 47, 82
Luke, 82

Macedonia, 19, 22, 52, 54, 61, 64
Malta, 85
marriage, 47, 99
Miletus, 78, 82
mystery religions, 87-88, 89, 94, 103, 104

Nero, 85, 94

Onesimus, 91

pagan, paganism, 41, 47, 57, 64
papyrus, 9-11
"pastoral" letters, 104
Peter, 34, 44, 50
Philemon, Letter to, 87, 91-92, 94
Philippi, 51, 52, 54, 56, 98
Philippians, Letter to, 51-55
Phoebe, 80
Phrygia, 31
Priscilla, *see* Aquila
prisons, 51, 52, 85, 86, 87, 90

resurrection, of believer, 20, 48-49, 71
   of Christ, 15, 49, 71
Roman authorities, 25-26, 51, 82-83, 85, 94
Roman roads, 32, 64-66

Romans, Letter to, 64, 66, 68-69, 71, 73-77, 78-80
Rome, 15, 40, 64-66, 67, 69, 70, 77, 86, 91

Silas, 13, 17, 19, 20
Stephanas, 44, 46
synagogue, preaching in, 15, 17, 24-25, 28, 29

Tertius, 78, 81
Thessalonians, First Letter to, 17, 19-23
   Second Letter to, 24, 27-28, 29
Thessalonica, 13, 17, 19, 20, 21, 26, 43
Timothy, 13, 17, 19, 20, 21, 23, 41, 53-54, 57, 81, 101, 103
Timothy, Letters to, 101, 104, 106
Titus, 25, 34, 60, 61, 101, 103
Titus, Letter to, 101, 104
tradition, 28
travel, in Roman times, 13, 14, 31, 32, 81, 82, 85
Troas, 60, 82
Tychicus, 91, 96

Venus, *see* Aphrodite

widows, 104

DESIGNER—*Giorgetta Bell*
TYPE—*12/13 Cornell Fotosetter*
TYPESETTER—*Parthenon Press*
MANUFACTURER—*Parthenon Press*
PRINTING PROCESS—*Offset, 1 color*
PAPER—*70# Children's Text*
END SHEETS—*70# Beckett Text*
BINDING—*Holliston's Kingston, natural finish*